Printed in the United States of America

First Edition 2003

ISBN 0-9724925-1-8

10 9 8 7 6 5 4 3 2 1

Cover and Book Design
by *Nasser Sleem*
Design Assistance
by *Laura Hughes*
Website
www.arcone.com
Email
info@arcone.com

THE TREND COMMANDMENTS™

Turning Cultural Fluency into Marketing Opportunity

LARRY SAMUEL

NEW YORK
CITY

ACKNOWLEDGMENTS

Thanks to all the reference librarians at the New York Public Library, Jefferson Market branch, and to all the journalists who are out there on the front lines writing the first draft of history. Much thanks to the dozens of coffee shop personnel who served up my daily grandes. This book would not have been possible without you or, at the very least, would have been a lot duller. Thanks also to David Levy, Tom Pahl, and all the fellas in Washington Square Park, the latter who encouraged me to keep writing while illustrating their particular brand of laissez faire capitalism.

Kudos to designers extraordinaire Nasser Sleem and Laura Hughes at Arc-1 Media, (www.arcone.com), photographer Ken Burnstein, and to Katherine Watson and all the other fine folks at BookMasters. Finally, much love to Mary Ellen and to my mom, who each continue to inspire me every day.

CONTENTS

Contents

INTRODUCTION

Welcome to the real land of milk and honey. Moses was without a doubt the go-to guy when it came to delivering messages from the CCO (Chief Creation Officer) and making travel plans but he was no marketing genius, trust me. *The Trend Commandments*™ is your passport out of the cultural wilderness leading to a promised land of marketing opportunities. This book will offer you a new vocabulary or language to speak in the marketplace and show you how to apply these conversation skills to your business. Think of it as a way to raise your C.Q. (Cultural Quotient) in order to be in the right place at the right time with the right ideas.

The main reason I wrote this book was to pass on my learnings from my years as a leading trend consultant to Fortune 500 companies and major ad agencies. A big part of my mission is to try to shrink the sea of confusion and misunderstanding surrounding trends, which has only seemed to get worse in recent years. Many people believe trends to be about the latest, the hippest, the coolest, tipping us off to what's in versus out, what's hot versus cold, what's new versus old. The truth is that most trends are in fact not cool (or even "trendy") at all, having little or nothing to do with the fashion, hairstyle, band, or drink of the moment. Trends are exponentially more democratic, populist, and, most importantly, opportunistic and leverageable than coolness. To put it another way, coolness is the guy or gal you date for kicks but trends are whom you take home to mom and dad (or to your board of directors). Thinking of trends as fleeting, ephemeral, and superficial fluff has also contributed to the wrong idea that they are ends to themselves when trends are much more often a means to a greater end. Part of your mission, this book will show, will be to develop a good sense of "trendar"—trend radar to filter out the lightweights and pretenders from the real thing and to use as a compass or GPS to point you in the right direction.

Too often equated with the lifestyles of leggy supermodels or teenagers with too much time and/or money on their hands, trends are actually an integral, vital component of any society. Because of our youthcentric society, progressive orientation, and insatiable appetite for "The Next Big Thing," however, the true value and significance of trends has largely been lost. Trends reveal the seminal patterns or themes of a society, telling us where that society is headed, what it aspires to become. They both reflect and shape a culture and serve as key symbols of our individual and collective identities. Trends are directional indicators or beacons that form a cultural arc or trajectory and help us anticipate what's next. They allow us to connect the scattered dots of society, to make sense out of the cultural mayhem, and, most importantly, to make (the right) decisions. When stacked together (*vis-a-vis* these ten commandments), trends are an immensely powerful strategic and tactical resource but they are often underused and misused. The most common mistake is to see trends as isolated, rather random phenomena and not part of a complex web of connections and relationships. Versus our regular and I think unhealthy habit of dividing, segmenting, and differentiating groups from other groups and individuals from other individuals, trends also represent an inclusive, holistic way to view society and the marketplace. They cross demographic boundaries with reckless abandon, mocking the social divisions of age, gender, race, ethnicity, class, and geography we like to construct. Trends also frequently skirt political party lines, making the ideological labels of "liberal" and "conservative" seem monolithic and silly. And unlike what people say, think, or say they think, trends are real, serving as hard, tangible evidence and firm proof of our cultural priorities. One may (and should) argue about a trend's social significance and marketing implications, in other words, but one can't challenge its existence.

As a working definition, consider a trend to be nothing more (and nothing less) than a particular expression or articulation of a society's values which is in ascent, i.e., rising in popularity, status, worth, and power. Trends can be seen as tips of cultural icebergs, relatively small chunks floating on the surface of society that should warn you there is probably something much bigger underneath. Switching metaphors faster than you can say *Titanic 2*, they are the strands of a society's DNA, the structural design of a culture's gene pool and a vital clue to who we are as a social organism. Or, to once again switch metaphors at the risk of your returning this book and ordering the one you really wanted, you know, the one with the pictures of famous people's dogs, trends are like leaves on our cultural tree which sprout, change color and shape, and eventually die. Like any living thing, each one is unique and has a lifecycle all its own. Trends vary dramatically in importance and scope, ranging from a blip on the radar to a full-fledged social movement. Their "horizontality," i.e., pervasiveness, popularity, and ubiquity, is, I believe, even more important than their verticality, i.e., how long they have been around. Because of their fluidity, however, trends often overlap, mimicking the chaotic nature of the culture they signify. They are, essentially, a mess, the very reason why few people understand how to use them as a marketing tool.

Hence *The Trend Commandments*™. This book is designed to give you a framework or structure by which to ground your brands in the cultural zeitgeist and help you choose which battles to fight. The ten commandments are, I believe, the synthesis or distillation of our cultural soup, the concentrated essence of where we are and where we're headed. They are rules to follow (and occasionally break) in order to be in sync (versus 'N Sync) with the cultural flow based on trends from across society. Each of the commandments is a building block of our cultural foundation and, not coincidentally, part and parcel of the American experience, steeped in our history and always present in some way. If each trend is an individual strand of our cultural DNA, consider the ten commandments in this book a "cultural genome project," detailing the genetic code of American culture at its cellular level (and, because of our empire-like status rivaling ancient Rome or Greece, that of much of the world). Again, my goal is not so much to inform you of new trends (which are easily found) as much as to help you become more culturally fluent and recognize ways to translate that fluency into business opportunities. Because most trends in the foreseeable future should fall into one or more of the ten commandments (the more a trend overlaps commandments, the stronger the trend), *The Trend*

Commandments™ is what I believe to be the skeleton key to marketing success in the 21st century.

The best way to use this book is to consider each of the one hundred trends and ten commandments within the context of your brand, company, category, and industry. Focus more on the commandments rather than the individual trends, as the latter are essentially ways to illustrate the cogency and validity of the former. Use the Opportunity statements at the end of each trend and the industry-specific "Ka-Ching!" statements at the end of each chapter as one way, and just one way, to translate the information into an actionable idea. Think of them as fodder to create your own new business, strategic planning, new product, positioning, advertising, or promotion ideas based on your own corporate mission, company assets, brand equities, and marketing initiatives. Before you know it, opportunities of epic, biblical proportions may very well appear before you like a bolt from heaven. Hallelujah!

1
TREND COMMANDMENT

Stir Passion.

TREND COMMANDMENT 1
Stir Passion.

How do you pick your marketing battles in our post-modern, post-everything culture? Do people have anything in common in our sliced and diced society? What the hell, I'll go and ask it: What's the meaning of life? One word: passion. Passion consists of ideas, events, activities, or pursuits that are grounded in powerful emotions. More passionately, so to speak, you get that unmistakable feeling in your gut, that sense of something resonating on a decidedly visceral level. Passion is larger than life, bigger than any individual, transcending the ordinary. Whether steeped in spirituality, desire, love, loss, or fear, passion is like a cultural power surge, a concentrated source of social energy which touches our collective nerve. Despite the economic downturn, many of us can still afford to pursue our passions after a full generation of prosperity, which is the true definition of luxury. Passions say who you are not only to others but to yourself, a siren of one's identity.

From a marketing standpoint, the wonderful thing about passion points is that they are fundamentally universal, cutting across all demographics and functioning as common denominators we all share but, of course, express quite differently. Because they tap into strong feelings, passion almost always lead to business opportunity, as all great success stories are somehow based in a deep emotional connection. And because passion is blissfully ignorant of our obsession with dividing people into different segments, they serve as a form of cultural Esperanto that can plug directly into any marketing plan or brand strategy. An alternative way to think about marketing, in fact, is as the challenge or opportunity to identify sources of passion among consumers and to then make your product or service part of that passion. Here then are some sites of passion that are in cultural ascent, i.e., rising in both popularity and power, to point you in the passionate direction.

INVESTING: Socially Responsible Funds

Good news for more passionate investors: making money and doing the right thing are not necessarily ships passing in the night. Since 1971, do-gooders have been putting their money where their hearts are by refusing to help finance corporations that pollute the environment, test products on animals, sell tobacco, or commit other such nasty acts. Instead, socially responsible investors proactively back companies that are good corporate citizens by hiring minority or women managers, being labor-friendly and environmentally conscious, and following vigilant accounting practices. According to a report by the Weisenberger Funds, socially responsible investments (SRIs) have grown five times faster than all other kinds of mutual funds over the past 30 years, proof positive that consumers are increasingly inscribing investing with a conscience. There are now about 200 such funds with total assets of over $100 billion, making SRIs account for a decent-sized piece of America's investment pie. In fact, the Social Investment Forum estimates that one out of every $8 that is professionally managed in the United States is an SRI. And best of all, SRIs have been very competitive with other funds, performing equal to or better than their cousins from across the tracks. The leaders in the field—Calvert, Domini, Citizens, Meyers, and Green Century—have all generated between 10% and 20% growth on a 10-year average. Fund managers use "negative screens" to weed out the bad guys and "positive screens" to identify the good guys which, in our post-Enron and -WorldCom world, now include factors such as reasonable executive compensation and auditors without conflicts of interest. SRIs are more relevant and popular than ever not only in the wake of corporate scandals but as a result of a broad post-9/11 awakening that there is more to life than money. The fact that SRIs tend to experience less of a hit during an economic downturn than other funds because investors are less likely to bail when the bears come to town has certainly contributed to making some of big boys of the investing world, like Morgan Stanley, jump on the trend. As well, because companies in SRI funds tend to follow "best practices" policies in their respective industry, their performance over the long term is typically better than average. Ethical management, in short, usually shows up in the bottom line over the long haul. As it becomes easier to check out companies' records on social, environmental, and ethical issues on websites such as CorporateRegister.com and SocialFunds.com, look for more Americans to dive into the socially responsible investment pool.

Invest passion in your products and services in order to make the world a richer place.

INHERITANCE : Ethical Wills

Social responsibility and inheritance are meeting head-on as many of us realize that there is an opportunity, perhaps even an obligation, to leave our loved ones something more than that 64-piece Haviland Limoge china set complete with gravy boat. The hottest thing in estate planning is the ethical will, a document intended to pass on one's "philosophical wealth," personal insights, and life rules collected over the years. Complementing traditional wills which bestow financial assets and material possessions to one's heirs, ethical wills are bequests of a less tangible but often more valuable sort—a portfolio of values, principles, memories, and advice. More and more Americans are infusing the dry-as-a-bone, all-business estate planning process with passion, wanting to ensure that their legacy consists of more than a wad of dough and bunch of chatzkes. Baby boomers especially are attracted to the idea, drawing upon their idealistic counterculture roots to realize that there are more important things than that Sub-Zero refrigerator and collection of Napa Valley's best. Ethical wills are actually a very old idea, found in both the Old and the New Testaments. Like Jacob, Moses, and Jesus, latter-day saints (and no doubt sinners) want to leave a record of their unique set of footprints in the sand and a roadmap for their family and friends to follow for the future. Those who prepare ethical wills often share them with their heirs while they're still around, a trend accelerated after 9/11 when many of us gained a greater appreciation of life's unpredictability and fragility. Ethical wills, in written form ranging in length from a paragraph to a Stephen King novella (and sometimes on audio- or videotape), typically include a telling of one's family history and life story, and the lessons learned along the way. Books and kits are readily available as guides for the DIYer (check out EthicalWill.com), and professional help too is around for those who want it. Specialists in the growing field charge $2,500 to $10,000 to prepare an ethical will, and lawyers and financial planners are increasingly offering the service to their clients. As some 70+ million boomers start to make plans for the big Woodstock festival in the sky, expect ethical wills to be a hefty part of what gets left to Generations X and Y.

Find a way that your product or service can help consumers let others know that they were indeed here.

ONLINE:
Interactive Grief

"When it seems that our sorrow is too great to be borne, let us think of the great family of the heavy-hearted into which our grief has given us entrance, and inevitably, we will feel about us their arms, their sympathy, their understanding."—Helen Keller

And where are the heavy-hearted who have already experienced the loss of a loved one increasingly going for sympathy and understanding? To any of a number of websites dedicated to help those on their "grief journey." Those in need of spiritual and emotional healing in bereavement are finding it online, crying on someone's virtual shoulder any time they feel they need to. These literal sites of passion help mourners work through their loss and find comfort and solace by giving them permission to grieve. The first interactive grief site ("Serving the Web Since 1995"), WebHealing.com is run by Tom Golden, a DC-based psychotherapist. In addition to a discussion page and "honor page," the site offers audio grief workshops to help visitors through their crises. Another site, GriefNet.org, has no less than 37 e-mail support groups, and includes KIDSAID, a page for kids to find information, ask questions, and share their grief. Along with a group of volunteers, the non-profit site is managed by Cendra Lynn, Ph.D., a Michigan-based clinical grief psychologist, death educator, and "traumatologist." At Groww.com, visitors "find partners in pain sharing their experience and strength." Calling itself "an independent haven for the bereaved developed by the bereaved," the site claims to consist of "the most loving people on the Internet for all who are grieving." Start in grief recovery, then move to the chat branches, discussion forums, inspirational writings, and memorial pages. The granddaddy of them all, however, is AARP with its interactive grief site (AARP.org/griefandloss). A "community of care," AARP offers books, workshops, and programs like how to create an online journal to express feelings of grief and loss. In addition to its online discussion board to post grief-related questions, express one's feelings and experiences, and share insights with others, AARP also provides a grief support line (1-866-797-2277) for callers wanting to talk to "someone who cares." This rather new form of grieving is changing the way we deal with death, moving the process from an exclusive, private affair among family and friends to an inclusive, public one made up of strangers. Count on all kinds of passion to be shared online.

Give strangers the opportunity to find each other (and passion) on your web site.

SPORTS:
Fantasy Leagues

Bottom of the ninth. Bases loaded. Two outs. Full count. And you're managing the team. Just a fantasy? Not for the millions of folks in sports fantasy leagues who get to compete against each other using real games, real players, and real data in real time. 15% of Americans over 18 have participated in a fantasy league, according to *Sports Illustrated*, all of them living in a parallel universe composed of statistics and standings. Each league is a passionate online community where members battle it out using professional baseball, football, or basketball players as their pawns. For newbies, here's how it works: from their digital dugouts, Steinbrenner wannabees go to sites like Jackpot.com, CBSSportsline.com, or MLB.com to assemble a team of players (while staying within the salary cap). Then they wait for their players to perform in real games and, before you can sing "Take Me Out to the Ballgame," move up or down in the league's standings based on their guys' whacks or whiffs. What's amazing about sports fantasy leagues is the amount of information available to make the right (or wrong) decisions and the dedication among members to use that information. Every statistic imaginable on every big league player can be and is used to get a competitive edge, with league members studying harder to choose their players than they did for their SATs. Sports fantasy leagues have become very big business, with scads of both online and offline sources to supply arm-chair managers with pre-crunched numbers, draft lists, strategies, ratings, forecasts, insider information, and cheat sheets. NASCAR too is now in the fantasy league game, offering subscribers on its web site the chance to pit their team of drivers against thousands of others, and even professional fishing has thrown its line into the fantasy lake. The next generation of sports fantasy leagues will use interactive television to allow viewers to compete against each other by collecting points for their players' performance. What's the big draw of fantasy leagues? Just as in the other great American pastime—the stock market—the Internet is allowing users to get in the game rather than just watch the professionals from the sidelines. Now that's a field of dreams!

Allow your customers to be players versus spectators when it comes to making purchase decisions.

WORK :
Office Romances

At work, the hottest fantasy is no longer that we're all going to get rich from the Internet but, more often than not, that hottie at the copy machine. Office romances are blooming, as more employers look the other way when Cupid shoots his arrow in the workplace. 75% of U.S. companies, in fact, have no policy at all when it comes to fraternizing with that guy or gal in the next cubicle. (One that does is Wal-Mart, which prohibits store managers and hourly employees from co-mingling.) Many companies are not only tolerating but encouraging what once was quite the taboo, believing that employees who play together are less likely to stray to competitors. Even sometimes crusty human resource managers understand that some playing of footsie under the conference table is inevitable when you put a bunch of people who share common career interests in close quarters for long hours. Despite the danger and intrigue surrounding an office fling, many believe that hooking up with someone you already know something about is a safer romantic route than the randomness of blind dates, dating services, or pick-ups. One study found that a full third of all romances begin at work, not too surprising considering that, for many, one's social life revolves around work. Another recent study bears out that roses are red, violets are blue, when they're at work, many do pitch woo. A 2002 *Elle* magazine/MSNBC.com poll found that 62% of those surveyed reported having had at least one fling at work. A whopping 41% claimed to have had sex while at work, with 16% of workers deciding for some reason to collaborate in the boss's office (watch that pen and pencil set!). 7% of the survey got caught in *coitus uh-oh-erruptus*, most of whom likely fell into the 19% who reported that their office liaison was a mistake. Still, a full 25% said that they had met their current partner at work, suggesting that despite the more serious risks (e.g., sexual harassment suits) and mild annoyances (e.g., the occasional smooching in the elevator), office romances are an increasingly legitimate place to begin a relationship in our work-centric society. Look for the workplace to continue to heat up as more bosses recognize that a happy employee is usually a good employee.

Bring passion to your marketing party by making your brand part of a love connection.

RELATIONSHIPS:
Same-Sex Marriages

Whether having met at work or elsewhere, what could be more passionate than the ties that bind two people? And the most passionate spot in the passion-filled sea of relationships is the intensifying battle over the very definition of marriage. Gay and lesbian rights activists are challenging the idea that marriage is the exclusive domain of heterosexuals and, bit by bit, succeeding in their quest. Vermont's civil unions law, California's domestic partnership bill, and Hawaii's reciprocal beneficiary status are all steps in a long march towards the possible legalization of same-sex marriages. More and more gay and lesbian couples are suing states for the right to marry and be awarded full and equal estate claims, medical benefits, and other protections and privileges that heterosexuals enjoy. And gay couples are now happily mugging in Sunday's Styles section of *The New York Times*, an important endorsement of same-sex partnerships that will no doubt have a trickle-down effect upon public sentiment. Other countries, including Germany, Finland, Portugal, and Denmark are gradually recognizing same-sex partnerships from a legal perspective, and the Netherlands recently became the first country in history to allow gay and lesbian couples full marriage rights. Conservatives, of course, are puling their straight hair out, arguing that marriage between a man and a woman is the bedrock of civilization, the institution which keeps society together. They blame same-sexers for "cheapening" marriage, arguing that tolerance for alternative lifestyles is one thing but redefining the concept of the institution for everyone is quite another. But traditionalists forget that marriage is indeed a fluid concept that has changed over the years. Not that long ago, wives were considered legal property, with no more rights than the cow in the shed or the horse in the barn. And until 1866, marriage in the U.S. was strictly a white affair (many may be shocked to learn that blacks and whites could not marry in all 50 states until 1967). Battening down the connubial hatches, some 35 states have passed laws that do not recognize same-sex marriages and, with its 1996 Defense of Marriage Act, Congress (and President Clinton) went on the record that the only legal union in our union is that between a man and a woman. As victories in local and state courts nibble away at federal law, however, and as a more gay-friendly generation comes into positions of power (58% of college freshman believe homosexual marriages should be legal, according to a 2002 *USA Today* poll), expect the bedrock of civilized society to experience some seismic quakes.

Hitch your marketing wagon to the passion surrounding any and all forms of committed relationships.

SECURITY :
Spy Gear

Look up. Is there a camera watching your every move? You never know these days, as the evil twins of passion, fear and paranoia, trigger a take-no-prisoners lovefest with all things surveillance. With the end of the Cold War, manufacturers of spy gear re-tooled for the consumer market and are now finding a sizable audience eager to protect themselves from...whatever. After 9/11, spy toys instantly became anti-terrorism devices, making this category one of the hottest in an otherwise ho-hum retail environment. Stores such as The Counter Spy Shop, Spy Tech, iSpy, and Espionage Unlimited are doing gangbuster business, bringing safety and security gadgets worthy of James Bond's "Q" to the masses. Mini-surveillance cameras (better take a close look at that wall clock) start at $100, but it's the $500 Teddy Bearcam you want if you're not too sure about your nanny or babysitter. How to keep the barbarians at the gate? How about a $195 driveway alert system or, should that fail, a $115 electronic dog whose bark gets louder as the perp gets closer. For the bravehearts who dare to occasionally leave their homes, bulletproof vests are *de rigeor* (fashionistas might opt for the $1,800 bulletproof leather jacket). Accessorize that antiballistic

schmata with Casio's Wrist Camera Watch ($249 list, $199 for bargain hunters). The color digital camera stores 80 images, can transfer pictures to a computer, and incidentally, tells pretty good time. For the more serious who want to be in like Flint, Night Owl Optics will make you hoot with joy. The NYC company offers 19 different night-vision products, from binoculars to monoculars to goggles, starting at $150. Just visit your local Wal-Mart or Costco and you too will soon be seeing things that go bump in the night. International men and women of mystery will want even more high-tech gear, like American Technology's HyperSonic Sound System which lets you throw your voice to confuse your enemies or CCS International's Tracking Transmitter which allows you to reveal your whereabouts anywhere on the planet (within a mile) from your belt buckle or shoe heel. As concerns about our and our family's personal safety are shaken (not stirred), I spy more of us turning into real life Maxwell Smarts and 007s in search of greater security.

Empower consumers by positioning your product or service as a weapon against real or perceived enemies.

TECHNOLOGY: Privacy Rights

"They that give up essential liberty to obtain a little temporary safety deserve neither liberty nor safety." —Benjamin Franklin

The flip side to safer living through technology is, of course, a full-scale assault on our inalienable rights to privacy. In a perfect example of the contradictions sewn into our cultural quilt, we are passionate about both security and privacy, and want more of each even though they make strange bedfellows. As Big Brother makes his hunky presence known in both public and private arenas, however, privacy is more often the one squeezed out of bed. Wiretaps were up 25% in 2001 versus 2000, according to the Administrative Office of the United States Courts, and random drug-testing at work and school are increasingly becoming the golden rule. Telemarketers and direct mailers literally know where we live and, with employee background checks, the theme of the workplace is more often becoming "I Know What You Did Last Summer." Even if you're a current employee, it's perfectly legal for your company to dig up your credit reports, civil court records, criminal records, and even driving records going back ten years or more. But it's the online world that arguably presents the biggest threat to the very American idea and ideal of personal privacy. Spammers, mass e-mailers, and e-snoops can find a way into your in-box if they really want to, and there's talk of using consumer databases to identify potential security risks. Collected data such as buying patterns, religious affiliation, medical history, and magazine subscriptions may one day be shared with Uncle Sam to help determine if you're one of the bad guys.

70% of online consumers say they are worried about online privacy, a June 2002 Jupiter Research report found, but most are willing to swap personal information for a chance to win a C-note. Not helping matters is that more than half of web surfers use the same screen name and password on all the sites they visit, making it easier for digital busybodies to track your every electronic move. Adding to this Orwellian nightmare is all the technology being developed or used in the name of homeland security. Video information, lie detectors, biometric cards, retinal and fingerprint scans, automatic face recognition, and electronic body scanners that see through clothing (yikes!) are all ways to make our country and the world a safer place but at a high cost.

As our fundamental right to life, liberty, and the pursuit of happiness continues to clash with the greater need for national security, expect a full-fledged privacy movement to begin to boil and bubble.

Help consumers keep others from unnecessarily knowing what goes on behind their closed doors.

COLLECTING : Rare Books

With the mantra of the new millennium being "microchips ahoy!," the first rule of collecting—whatever runs against (versus with) the cultural stream typically increases in value—is more apropos than ever. And with nothing running faster these days than digital information, smart collectors are wisely counting on distinctly analog objects and experiences to rise in demand and worth. The rare book is a perfect example, laughing in the general direction of everything the Information Age represents. Works of art and in limited supply, rare books are rather ironically becoming the collectible du jour in our era when many of us spend much of our days staring at computer screens. Celebrities like Johnny Depp have caught the bibliophile bug, drawn to the pure aesthetics and downright anachronistic nature of a high-quality, hard to find text. One doesn't have to be Depp-like, however, to collect rare books. In fact, the investment aspects of collecting books should be considered less important than the sheer love of owning (and reading) a beautiful object. More of us are realizing there is nothing quite like holding a real, well-made book, offering a palpable experience that is augmented when one imagines who may have held the very thing over the course of decades or centuries. Once you've had a leather bound, handmade book in your grubby hands, you'll never feel the same way about a contemporary mass market paperback with its crammed in type, acidic paper, and second-grade glue. Interestingly, age is not an especially relevant factor in determining the value of a book, as the recent surge in first edition Harry Potter books makes clear (better have at least 20,000 clams in your pocket to score one of those). The book's historical or literary significance, whether it's a first edition, its condition, and some other factors (like whether it was suppressed) are the most important criteria for shaping relative demand. But it is the thrill of the hunt that makes book collectors foam at the mouth, the pursuit of that obscure volume on South American plant life, the Boer War, or Abraham Lincoln's clothes. That hunt has been made a lot easier over the last few years with the shifting of the rare book buying and selling universe online. Just go to eBay or sites like Bookbarn.com and you too may soon be scouring the shelves of the global bookstore for a literary masterpiece. Take a page from rare book collecting as we try to build a personal library of passion.

Tap into the power and the passion of high-touch in our high-tech times.

TRANSPORTATION :
Custom Motorcycles

"A good bike appeals to your reason. A great bike appeals to your emotions."—Cyril Huze, custom motorcycle builder

Think a Harley is the epitome of vehicular passion? Think again. Those who really want to be high on the hog are choosing custom motorcycles—one-of-a-kind cruising bikes that are personally commissioned and individually built. Cruisers are the heavyweight division of the motorcycle category, big bikes with high handlebars and a V-twin engine which sounds like hell on wheels. The leader of the pack in the cruiser market is, of course, Harley-Davidson, who pigs out with about a 42% share. But for some easy riders, Harley is now too middle-of-the-road, ridden by lots of rebel wannabees just playing bad boy dress-up. Unlike assembly linebuilt Harleys, custom bikes are hand-made by companies who are as passionate about choppers as their customers. Cyril Huze's shop in Boca Raton, Florida, for example, is a self-described "dream factory," turning out no more than a dozen bikes per year. "Passion is the engine of creativity," says Huze, combining "guts, brains, and soul" to create customized models with names like

Surreal Huze, Dreamliner, and Stardust. Exile Cycles of Sun Valley, California is also "a company built on passion," selling custom bikes for $25,000 to $50,000, about the same as a Harley. Big Dog Motorcycle of Wichita, Kansas lets you "build your dream dog" by choosing paint colors and accessories from six different models (Wolf, Bulldog, Mastiff, Boxer, Husky, and Pitbull) and Victory Motorcycles too lets potential customers have it their way. Through Victory's Custom Order Program, little piggies get to build their own bike by providing specs such as colors, wheels (cast or laced), and tires (blackwall or whitewall) and then selecting from an array of chrome options and touring packages. More than 500 options can be selected for Victory's Touring Cruiser and 320 options for its Classic Cruiser, in fact, allowing riders to stand out from the rest of the two-wheel pack. Don't let the motorcycle business hog the passion of one-of-a-kind products and services.

Stir passion by coming up with ways to let consumers have it their way.

TREND COMMANDMENT 1
Stir Passion.

KA-CHING!

AUTOS
Present driving in your cars as a unique, passionate experience.

BEAUTY
Define beauty not as appearance but as a passion for life your product or service will add to.

ENTERTAINMENT & MEDIA
Raise the emotional quotient of your products and services to bring out the passion in your audience.

FASHION
Recast style as passion in the form of clothing.

FINANCE
Express financial goals in terms of the passion they will help consumers realize.

FOOD & BEVERAGE

Leverage the inherent passion of eating and drinking by positioning your brand as a sensory adventure.

HEALTHCARE

Communicate that your product or service delivers life's most precious gift—wellness.

RETAIL

Position your store as the place to find that which brings each shopper his or her personal passion.

TECHNOLOGY

Focus not on your brand's bells and whistles but on how it can help make the user's life a little (or a lot!) better.

TRAVEL & HOSPITALITY

Pitch your product or service as a must-stop along life's passionate journey.

TREND COMMANDMENT 2

Spark Creativity.

TREND COMMANDMENT 2
Spark Creativity.

Would you rather be writing than reading right now? If so, you're not alone. The dynamics of popular culture appear to shape-shifting as more people demand to participate in its production rather than just its consumption. Creativity is rising in cultural status as the arts become more democratic, populist, and accessible, not limited to a few geniuses with God-given ability. Although the cult of celebrity remains as powerful as ever for our Hollywood royalty, America is becoming not unlike a developing nation where everyone gets to bang a drum or participate in the tribal hokey-pokey. Boomers especially are getting in touch with their creative side, rediscovering some early talent or exploring some activity they always wanted to and now can afford. As with much of emerging culture, technology is having a ricochet effect, causing more of us to seek sanctuary from life.com and do things with our hands not involving double-clicking. Creativity is also nature's Prozac, known to kick in the endorphins and seratonin, making time and troubles temporarily disappear. Try to make a mosaic that won't fall apart and I guarantee you'll forget all about that joke of a bonus or even how your dog just ate your favorite Cole-Haans.

Creativity is especially fertile soil for marketers to sow, steeped in self-expression and aspiration (who doesn't want to be more creative?). As the wellspring for many if not most trends, the universe of creativity is also society's petri dish, with artists of all stripes less inclined to tow the consensus line and less afraid to take risks and try new things. From the turn-of-the-century Bloomsbury Group to the between-the-wars Bohemians to the postwar Beats to the counter-culture Mods to the late '70s Punks, the cream of the creative crop not only have been the avant garde but have made many of us wonder if we have any creative magic ourselves. Finding the answer to that question is one of contemporary culture's dominant themes, leading consumers to get creatively jiggy for both fun and profit. Here are some ways we're dancing around the creative fire in order to spark some creative marketing ideas.

BEAUTY :
Body Art

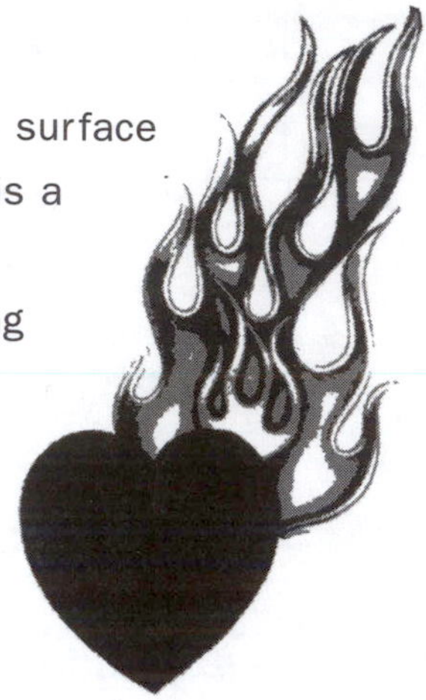

You don't even have to look under the surface of American culture to know that creativity is a big part of our body politic. A good many Americans—almost 1 in 6, in fact, according to an *American Demographics*/Harris Interactive survey—are tattooed and/or pierced, turning their own bodies into a walking, talking piece of art. Body art not surprisingly skews younger—the Mayo Clinic found that more than half of the students at one college in upstate New York were pierced and almost one fourth tattooed—but is an equal opportunity adorner when it comes to gender and race. Those who've elected to dye or puncture their skin will tell you it's all about self-expression, to (literally) mark your identity to the outside world. Body art allows one to define his or her own beauty, to take some control over the genetic hand one has been dealt. As a trend, body art is the little engine that could, continually chugging along as new teens and more mainstreamers hop aboard. Although popularized in the 1990s (with tattoos appropriated from the working class and piercing lifted from gay culture), body art is hardly new. The ancient Egyptians and Celtic tribes were way into body décor, and piercing was quite the naughty rage during the Victorian era. You can thank (or blame) the bellybutton ring craze on Liv Tyler and Alicia Silverstone, who famously wore them in the 1995 Aerosmith video "Crazy." Whether denoting membership in a group, commitment to a person or cause, or faith in a divine spirit, body art is first and foremost an act of creativity. Color, design, shape, technique, and placement are all elements in the visual equation as body artists use their imaginations to complete their blank epidermal canvass. And for those whose artistic vision changes over time, there is, fortunately, an alternative to the relative permanence of tattooing. Mehndi, the ancient Indian and African art of painting the body with henna, is all-natural, pain-free, temporary (two to four weeks), and visibly endorsed by such superbabes as Madonna and Naomi Campbell. Despite the Britneyization of piercing and body art in general, much of the rebelliousness (and social stigma) surrounding it remains, which no doubt contributes to its cultural resiliency. Count on many of us to continue to accessorize our birthday suits with individual artistry.

Help consumers create and realize their own interpretation of their inner and outer selves.

Writing : Poetry Slams

What's the word in writing? One especially fertile site of wordy (and worldly) creativity is poetry. A true poetry movement is in the works, driven by folks' desire to have their individual voices heard. The tentacles of poetry reach far and wide, as poets from all over the world find each other to celebrate the art form. Poetry festivals are collectives of creativity, gatherings to literally spread the word. At the annual Austin International Poetry Festival, Greater Pittsburgh Poem Chase, and Los Angeles Poetry Festival, for example, wordsmiths spout off in bookstores, bars, and cafes in a public, communal rant. Creativity is oozing not only at these once-a-year events but every day through online venues like the Electronic Poetry Center, a portal into the digital world of e-poetry and poetics. The most interesting and controversial site of poetry culture, however, is the poetry slam. Around in this country since 1987, when Marc Smith held the first at the Green Mill in Chicago, poetry slams trace their roots back to the 1970s punk scene and, of course, the 1950s Beats. At slams held every week at places like the Mercury Lounge in Austin or the Cantab Lounge in Boston, poets compete with each other, often for cash and always for applause. The Spoken Word Poetry Series in Providence, RI, Worchester, MA and Burlington, VT is a stream-of-Yankee-consciousness, an

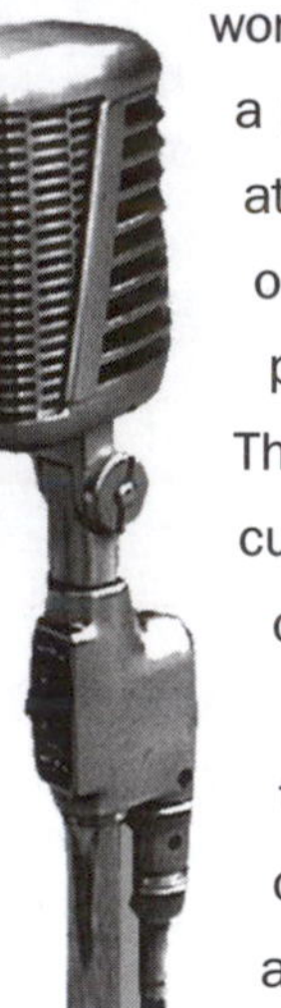

opportunity to be in the spotlight every week for three to ten minutes. An extreme form of poetry, slams are rowdy and raucous, and clearly influenced by another prime expression of creativity, rap. Political, personal, funny, and angry (sometimes and somehow simultaneously), a slam reading is, above all, a venting from the soul. Hardcore slammers meet at the annual National Poetry Slam, where some 50 teams battle it out in front of randomly chosen judges who use an Olympics-style scoring system. HBO saw the writing on the wall in early 2002, having big-time record producer Russell Simmons spin off his *Def Comedy Jam* stand-up series to create a few *Def Poetry Jam* shows. Hosted by rapper and actor Mos Def, the *Def Poetry Jam* brought together a culturally diverse group of young and established poets including Nikki Giovanni and Amiri Baraka with a few celebrity slammers like Jewel and Benjamin Bratt. Now the Jam is jamming on Broadway, as a group of poets called the "Voices of the Next America" take center stage. Watch poetry slams and other fertile breeding grounds of creativity spawn as we look for opportunities to let our inner voice ring out.

Speak up with products and services that allow consumers to express their creative sides.

EDUCATION : Music Lessons

Never got your chance to play "Freebird" in a garage band (or a song someone actually wanted to hear)? If so, don't fret. You can join the scores of other adults taking music lessons that were not part of your childhood experience or were abandoned for more frolicsome activities. The Music Teachers National Association reports that 25 to 55 year olds are the fastest growing group of new students, a great example of the rising cultural status of creativity among all age groups. Many are determined to fulfill a life ambition to be able to play a musical instrument (including one's voice), or simply approach it as an escape world or something to do just for kicks. Receiving musical lessons as a gift from one's spouse is also becoming increasingly popular, as what do you give your hubby when he's already got the Lexus, Ping titaniums, and subscription to *Men's Health*? Beginners typically find the first few lessons a humbling, frustrating experience, as the eye-hand coordination proves not to be what it used to be. But sooner or later old dogs learn some new tricks, and often find they have something to share which a child who is also learning how to tickle the keys, strum a guitar, or blow a horn.

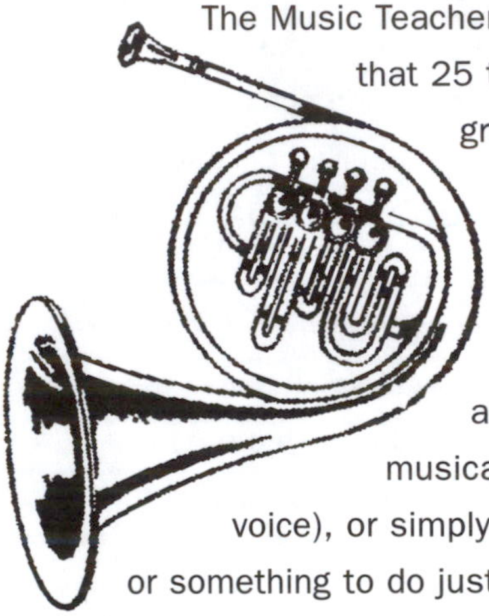

Besides the sudden surge in party invitations, research shows that learning how to play an instrument can sharpen thinking skills and perhaps even slow the aging process. And for those still living on Internet time, many teachers are happy to come to your office for an hour and run scales with you in a conference room. But lessons, many of them free, are also just a click away at a number of websites dedicated to keeping the hills alive with the sound of music. MusicPlay.com offers a "Virtual Music School" on its site, and WholeNote.com allows aspiring pickers to take online lessons contributed by the global guitar community. DrumBum.com claims its lessons to be "more fun than you can shake a stick at," while DrumLesson.com sells eight weeks of lessons (including 50 basic drumbeats!) for $15.95, about the cost of one CD. Trade groups such as the International Music Products Association (IMPA) are joining the chorus, helping adults find their inner Ozzie. The IMPA's New Horizons program gets instruments and instructions into the hands and hearts of over 60 groups of adults across the USA, while its Weekend Warriors program places musicians well over their teenage angst into rock bands. Hear the loud beat of adults wanting to get in tune with their creative selves.

Plug into products and services that allow consumers to develop their personal muse.

MUSIC : DJing & VJing

*"Each generation has its own soundtrack."—**DJ Spooky***

As rock 'n roll becomes eligible for AARP, DJing and VJing are offering a new generation a way to explore their creative chops. Professional DJing originated in late '60s Jamaican reggae and early hip-hop culture in the '70s and '80s, when ahead-of-the-curve cats like Kool Herc, Grand Wizard Theodore, and Mix Master Mike blazed the groovy trail. It would take, however, another 20 or so years before DJing became a legitimate and much sought after occupation, led by a group of highly paid, international superstars.

Top DJs like the tag-team of Sasha and Digweed and DJ Craze (who won the World DJ Championships in 1998, 1999, and 2000) spin, scratch, and do various and sundry other things to vinyl not recommended by the manufacturer. Club owners know that their bottom line relies heavily on the popularity of DJs and their ability to keep the crowd in the palms of their busy hands. Big-time DJs record their own CDs (check out the "United DJs of America" compilations), taking other peoples' music and literally turning it into a new art form. Whether carefully planned or improvised, a DJ's set is all in the mix, a making of something new out of many things old. The idea of sampling is at the heart of DJ Spooky's (a.k.a. Paul Miller) erudite philosophy of what he considers "social sculpture." As a "turntablist," DJ Spooky views the art as a kind of writing (phonograph literally means "sound writing"), cobbling disparate elements of music's past into something fresh, original, and unique. His collages of sound use music, voice, and computers, resulting in a life affirming joyful noise which reflects what he called in an interview in *Art Journal* our "cut-and-paste culture." We shouldn't be surprised that a generation so fragmented, technologically adept, and globally engaged has chosen as one of its principal art forms something that mirrors these same characteristics. Video jockeys too are using technology to blaze new trails of creativity, projecting images and animation onto huge screens in clubs, theaters, and concert arenas. Teched-out visual artists such as VJ Liquid.7 create moving wallpaper that pulses to the music that their DJ partners program, resulting in multimedia performances that hearken back to late sixties psychedelic light shows. DJs and VJs represent a new paradigm of art that is not fixed or static but rather, in DJ Spooky's words, "more about environments than just objects on the wall." Listen to the choice of a new generation as it redefines the very rules of creativity.

Put your own spin on the idea of sampling in your product category to turn consumers' heads.

DANCE:
Ballroom Dancing

For those who want to spin with their feet rather than with their hands, it's strictly ballroom. Ballroom dancing continues to pick up steam all over the world, sweeping people up with its romance, glamour, passion, and fun. Increasingly called "DanceSport," ballroom dancing is a creative fusion of time and place, bringing couples together not just face-to-face but cheek-to-cheek. For those needing a refresher course, Freds and Gingers get syncopated in either standard or Latin ballroom styles. Standard (or "modern") dances include the waltz, tango, foxtrot, and quickstep, while Latin styles include salsa, merengue, samba, rumba, cha-cha, and jive (the latter incorporating the various kinds of swing). Quite literally jump-started in the early '90s on the West Coast, swing has gradually bowed to more formal and classical styles not involving the tossing of one's partner over one's shoulder or, occasionally, across the floor. As the swing movement made clear, ballroom dancing is no longer limited to retirees waxing nostalgic for the good times at the Hollywood Canteen. More colleges are offering ballroom dancing for credit, and competitions among pre-teens are getting the millennium generation truly in sync. Terpsichoreans are also cutting an online rug at

BallroomDancers.com, learning new steps, taking lessons, listening to music, finding a place to dance or a partner, and buying and selling dance apparel. Within the ballroom community, a major battle is raging over whether it is an art or a sport, an important distinction not just to hoofers but for the International Olympic Committee. The IOC recognized ballroom dancing as a sport in 1997, and many hope that it will be included in the 2008 games in Beijing. The physical stamina required for ballroom dancing cannot be disputed; a single quickstep routine, for example, is equivalent to the energy expended in a 100-yard dash, and that's no jive. The other health benefits of ballroom dancing —improved balance, circulation, and body tone, as well as stronger bones—suggest that this is something baby boomers may be doing a lot of in the future to keep in shape when snowboarding becomes a bit too ambitious. Read these fascinating rhythms as a resounding refusal to be a creative wallflower.

Tap into the universal desire to celebrate life through creative expression.

COOKING:
Culinary Schools

What's cooking for a growing number of creative types? The culinary arts are hotter than a coal-stoked oven, offering an opportunity for aspiring chefs to put their money where diners' mouths are. Applications to and enrollment in culinary and hospitality schools are at record levels as artists whole palette is the palate decide to turn pro. From sea to shining sea, high school kids to ex-CEOs are earning certificates and degrees in fields like "pastry studies" in order to pursue careers in restaurants, catering, and hotels. Why are so many ready, willing, and able to stand the heat in the kitchen? The yeasty rise in the culinary arts are part of the general upswing in education, as ex-dot-commers and others downsized retrain for new careers. With interest in gourmet cooking higher than ever—a result of our increasingly discerning (and fussy) tastes—many see high-end food as a bouillabaisse of opportunity. But something much headier is going on as more of us seek to get in touch with our inner Emeril and explore our talent in a creative (and nurturing) medium. The rise in the prestige and status of chefs is also making more of us want to get our just desserts, especially for a younger generation whose role model is the yummier-than-a-buttermilkcrumpet Naked Chef. Even some doctors, lawyers, and financial chiefs are ditching their day jobs to jump in the culinary frying pan, attracted by the excitement (and unpredictability, as any food service worker can tell you) of the restaurant game. With this collective urge to don white aprons, schools and programs in the culinary arts are expanding and increasing in number. More and bigger classrooms are being added to existing schools, and new programs are being created to train people for the 2 million additional food service jobs that the National Restaurant Association forecasts will be available by 2010. Culinary arts programs increased 42% from 1997 to 2002 according to Shaw Guides, in fact, from 322 to 458. High (90%+) placement rates and multiple job offers are not unusual for graduates of such programs, although starting at the bottom ("Chop them onions!") is the port of entry for some during this time of slow (2-3%) growth in restaurant sales. One of the premier schools around is the French Culinary Institute in New York, where vittle sergeants teach future professionals (and some serious amateurs) no less than 250 basic competencies in Western food preparation. Students try out their fixins' at L'Ecole, the school's on-campus restaurant open to the public. Take a lesson from this pervasive desire to turn creativity into a recipe for success.

Offer consumers ways to cook up careers rich in creativity.

HOBBIES :
Woodworking

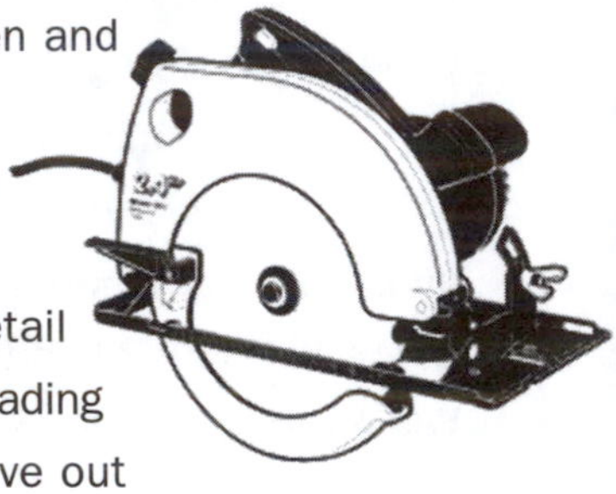

Creativity is also oozing out of the fingertips of millions of crafty types who find beauty and utility in the things they make themselves. With loads of advice from experts and often part of a social network, craftaholics have their busy hands doing everything from basket weaving to beeswax candle making to mosaic building. But for the craftiest craftsmen and craftswomen, there is no substitute for turning a piece of raw, buck-naked wood into something useful. Adult ed programs, community colleges, and retail stores are all chomping at the bit, spreading the woody word to those pining to carve out their creative niche. Women are the fastest growing demographic in woodworking, according to *Woodworker's Journal*, with the prestigious Rhode Island School of Design's furniture program turning out a new generation of woodchicks. Woodies typically start with smaller projects like toys or spice or magazine racks and work their way up to furniture, churning out desks, cabinets, tables, cribs, and entertainment centers. Whether using purchased plans, creating a custom design, or knocking off a store-bought, woodworkers find in the process the calming, therapeutic effects of focused handwork. Starting small and making mistakes along the way are perfectly acceptable, and even men are known to stop and ask questions when they are lost in Lumberland. In woodworking, as in most crafts, it's all about the tools. Blockheads gradually climb up the tool chain, adding band saws, table saws, jointers, planes, lathes, and dish and drum sanders as their skills improve. Safety first is the golden rule, with "measure twice, cut once" a close second. Working one's way up to "journeyman woodworker" is the ultimate pursuit for the hard core, although many are content to simply make the occasional bench, rocking chair, or acoustic guitar to keep or give away as a gift. The media have glommed onto woodworking like an oil-based stain, offering bits of how-to wisdom to do-it-yourselfers. *The American Woodworker* and *The New Yankee Workshop* (where master carpenter Norm Abrams holds court) are television shows aimed directly at wooda-couldas, and master of the house HGTV includes woodworking programming in its homey schedule. In new media, Woodworking.com is the oak of the e-forest, doling out advice in articles, chatting it up in forums, and offering links to other relevant sites. The leading magazine in the field, *Popular Woodworking*, is also online, giving out free project plans, reviewing new tools, and hosting a woodworker's book club. Woodworking is hard evidence of our longing for craft in our technological times, just one way many of us literally construct our identities.

Help consumers turn their ingrained creativity into reality.

HOME :
Landscape Design

For those wanting a bigger canvas on which to express their creativity, there's nothing like one's front or back yard. One of the great American pastimes—mowing the lawn—is going to seed as more of us chuck the old sod for more interesting terrain. Lawns that look not unlike the 9th hole at Augusta are being replaced or augmented with other grasses which have texture and movement and look good in all seasons. Green thumbs are putting that manicured, high maintainence Kentucky bluegrass out to pasture and in its stead throwing down a meadow of Indian grass, purpletop, big and little bluesterm, and even some grape vines and sumac. Unlike Kentucky blue which lays there year 'round like wall-to-wall carpet, reed and ornamental grasses and flowers can be a concert of sound and light, changing moods every hour and with every passing breeze. The essence of this new approach to landscape design is a greater sensitivity to what is indigenous to the region, i.e., what was there before humans set up camp. In the Midwest then, more yards are becoming prairie home companions as they were in their native, colonial state. In the Sunshine State, professional landscape designers like Raymond Jungles (seriously) are bringing back some of the tropical Florida wilderness by planting South American palm trees and Asian bamboo in client's yards. And in the California desert, more folks are cutting off thirsty lawns for the sculptural succulents and olive trees that thrived before the gringos came to town. Others are rescuing and promulgating heirloom varieties of flowers and vegetables through programs like Seed Savers Exchange. The net net is a more diverse, more sustainable ecological landscape truer to what the Master Gardener first had in mind. One leading landscape designer views this movement as analagous to restoring an old house, a going back to the floor plan laid out in the original architectural drawings. But the shifting plates in landscape design doesn't stop there. Those with their own vision of what their backyard should look like are bulldozing terra firma to forge a vista of earth, rock, and wild grass. Betcha your neighbor doesn't have a living sculpture behind his or her house. Even more aggressive lawnboys are creating "aquascapes" on their property, suburban oases complete with waterfalls, huge boulders, and ponds. These $3,000 to $100,000 grottos are right out of *Blue Lagoon* or *Fantasy Island*, sparing owners the cost and time of going to an expensive, distant private resort. Heed this urge to not just keep up with the Joneses but to make one's home different from every other kid's on the block.

Give consumers the seeds to let their creativity grow wild.

RETAIL :
Handmade Crafts

In our chain store age, where Mall X looks virtually identical to Mall Y and big box retailers rule from Portland, Maine to Portland, Oregon, where does one find things which look and feel different? To any number of offline and online stores selling items that have not rolled off an assembly line. Handmade crafts are flourishing as consumers search far and wide for objects that are one of-a-kind and, many believe, good-for-the-soul. A thriving artisanal sub-culture resides below the surface of the Mega-Mart retail landscape, creating things for everyday living while retaining the maker's personal touch. According to the Craft Organization Directors Association, some 127,000 Americans earn a living selling crafts, with combined annual sales of $14 billion. Like the Arts and Crafts movement of a century ago, today's handmade crafts movement insists on both form and function, that beauty and aesthetics should not come at the cost of usefulness and practicality. Crafts often combine traditional designs by Native American culture or ancient civilizations with new materials, bringing a best-of-both-worlds sensibility to the art form. From individuals or small production workshops and studios—the modern day equivalent to medieval guilds—come wearables, jewelry, furniture, tableware, and musical instruments made from wood, metal, glass, ceramics, textiles, and woven grass. Credit Dale Chihuly for melding the worlds of art and craft by redefining glass objects as sculpture. For those who can't afford a Chihuly water pitcher, there are plenty of other sources to find *object d'art* which you can and should actually use around the house. Brick-and-mortar stores like Ten Thousand Villages in Chesapeake, Virginia and other locations sell handmade objects from around the world and, best of all, are dedicated to paying fair wages to the artisans. Ebiza.com is probably the biggest seller of unique, handcrafted goods from points East and West, a global bazaar of furnishings, jewelry, and chatzkas. TheHitchinPost.com is the place to go for all things deerskin, while Broom-Shp.com is naturally where to get that handmade broom you've always wanted. Soap-StoneArtist.com features handcrafted carvings by the Inuits of Sanikiluaq, and FivePoleFarm.com specializes in handmade miniature flowerpot men made of terra cotta in Northampton, England. The list is, should there be any doubt, endless. Expect the relevance of handmade crafts to rise and rise as we fall deeper and deeper into the technological rabbit hole.

Offer consumers the ultimate form of creativity through hand-crafted artisanship.

TOURISM:
Creativity Themeparks

Picture yourself in a boat on a river with tangerine trees and marmalade skies. Step inside Crayola Works, Binny & Smith's 20,000 square foot interactive retail and studio experience in Arundel, Maryland (near Baltimore), and you might believe you indeed have kaleidoscope eyes. Leg-O may have set the bar of creativity themeparks for kids in the '90s with its Imagination Centers at Disneyland, Disneyworld, and the Mall of America, but Crayola Works seems to have raised it. The crayon company lays claim to creativity for kids, committed to help each and every young 'un think out of the box and discover his or her world through art. And with Crayola Works, which opened in June 2002, the company is offering kids full immersion in creativity, a magical journey sure to inspire their imaginations and sense of aesthetics. Purchase one of the nine activities kits (starting at $7.99) and before you can say, "Toto, I don't think we're in Kansas anymore," your little Van Gogh is headed down the "river of color." While painting soccer balls, making creepy-crawler condos, or decorating Frisbees, said artist-in-residence meets the obligatory cast of ultra-colorful characters which includes Perry Winkle, Aqua Marie, and Blizzard Blue (where are those funky orange-brown colors that all of us ditched or ate as kids?).

Should that temperamental creative genius prefer alternative media, point him or her to Chalk City or towards the mountain of Silly Putty, where he or she can, in the company's words, "face-morph." Parties too can be hosted at Crayola Works, where $9.99 per wee person buys a craft activity, game, goody bag, juice box, and cupcake (add two bucks for pizza). More than 60 "brand ambassadors" are there to motivate and encourage kids ("guests" in Disneyspeak) to go over the rainbow and realize their creative potential. Throughout the experience, kids are reminded that the process is more important than the results, something we could all keep in mind from time to time. Crayola Works is Binney & Smith's latest venture in living color, having sold more than 100 billion crayons in the century or so the company has been around. Now competing for kids' short attention span in an entertainment landscape of high-action video games, television, movies, and sports, the company has done an amazing job turning little sticks of wax into something much more. As creativity continues to be a quality we want to nurture in our kids, expect other companies to escort young consumers down the yellow (or Laser Lemon) brick road.

Make your brands more colorful by letting consumers play with them in creative, interactive settings.

TREND COMMANDMENT 2
Spark Creativity.

KA-CHING!

AUTOS
Swap 20th century standardization for 21st century craft in automobile design.

BEAUTY
Position beauty products and services as media by which consumers can create their own personal masterpiece.

ENTERTAINMENT & MEDIA
Give consumers the chance to be part of the creative process when they want to.

FASHION
Present your brands as not just something to wear but as an opportunity for consumers to express their creativity.

FINANCE
Bring left-brain creativity to right-brain analysis in packaging products and programs.

FOOD & BEVERAGE

View your food and beverage brands as edible creativity.

HEALTHCARE

Tell consumers that despite evidence to the contrary, a healthy body offers the best chance to have a creative mind.

RETAIL

Turn your store into an environment of creativity.

TECHNOLOGY

Define your brand's purpose as to help consumers become more creative people.

TRAVEL & HOSPITALITY

Develop a new segment in the travel and hospitality category: "creative tourism."

3
TREND COMMANDMENT

Declare Independence.

TREND COMMANDMENT 3
Declare Independence.

It's right there in our original mission statement. In the two centuries and change since declaring our independence, Americans have marched to the beat of a different fife and drummer. The notion of independence is ingrained in our cultural DNA, an essential part of who we are as a people and what differentiates from everyone else. Although many of us now take it for granted, independence was and remains a rather radical idea for both nations and individuals. Don't be fooled by their powdered wigs and petticoats. With their demand for life, liberty, and the pursuit of happiness, the founding fathers were rebels with a cause, forging a society in which citizens would be free from the tyranny of church and state.

The spirit of '76 lives on, of course, woven into the fabric of everyday life and our collective consciousness. We are not, as Jefferson imagined, a nation of yeoman farmers living off our private piece of land but self-sufficiency and self-reliance remain key markers of our communal and personal identities. Our inclination to create boundaries between "us" and "them" (can you say gated communities?) and to distance ourselves from the hoi polloi (how about private ambulances?) help define what it means to be American. Our very heroes—from Tom Paine to Honest Abe to James Dean to Rosa Parks to Steven Jobs—tend to be contrarians, people who challenged the status quo, took risks, and stood up for what they believed.

This strand of independence still courses through American culture, of course, challenging marketers to align themselves with consumers' indie instincts. Indie or alternative culture also almost always feeds mass or mainstream culture, functioning as a leading indicator of what will soon be considered conventional. Here are a few trends that declare our inherent desire to go our own way if and when we choose in order to get you headed down your indie trail.

JOURNALISM : Blogs

"The newspaper is a lecture. The Web is a conversation."—James Lileks, Minneapolis Star Tribune columnist and blogger

Revolution is certainly in the air in journalistic circles as blogs bring independence from and democracy to the media monarchy. Weblogs or blogs (also "Me-zines") are online daily observations about the news, media, politics, technology, entertainment, and anything and everything else, along with links to relevant sites. Most often using software by Pyra Labs (Pyra.com), bloggers rant and rave in real-time, sharing their admittedly biased take as if on a digital soap-box in an electronic town square. Everyone can be a pundit in the Blogosphere, an alternative media universe that spans far left, far right, and all points in between. Created by Internet writers in the late 1990s, blogs are rapidly being co-opted by mainstream media for their immediacy and ability to reach like-minded people. Journalist wannabees and real ones like Andrew Sullivan of *The New York Times Magazine* and Chris Matthews, Mr. Hardball on MSNBC, post daily weblogs, offering their personal points-of-view to create nothing less than a new form of journalism. With over half million blogs out there (and a new one created every 40 seconds), offline media have a new force to reckon with that never goes to sleep and is, even more important, interactive. Mix it up, for example, with Glenn Reynolds, one of the anchormen of the blog world. His website, InstaPundit.com (called "*The New York Times* of the bloggers" by *Pravda* and "The Grand Central Station of Bloggerville" by the *American Journalism Review*), gets 70,000 views a day by about 23,000 people and is a legitimate source for "real" journalists looking for a juicy quote, analysis, or opinion. With the snarfing up of blogger du luxe Micky Kaus by Microsoft's online magazine *Slate* and MSNBC ditching its discussion board for Weblog Central (a portal of links to blogs arranged by subject), the burgeoning empire of virtual journalism grows ever larger and more powerful. Many blogs, however, remain personal vanity sites, which represents their true power as an independent voice of the people not beholden to publishers, editors, and subscribers. With their ability to offer multiple dialogues, blogs are a social phenomenon that is exponentially more heterogeneous and chaotic than the traditional model of journalism that has been in place since Gutenberg booted up his printing press. As the wireless web expands the universe of the Blogosphere, expect the democratic ethos "the more voices the better" to flourish alongside our skeptical instincts to "let the surfer beware."

Adopt "we the people" as your motto by opening up the channels of communication with consumers.

EDUCATION :

Home & Charter Schools

Dissatisfied with what is or isn't being taught in America's often less than hallowed hallways, more parents are declaring independence from public schools. Both home schooling and charter schools are on the rise, a growing and legitimate movement reflecting the erosion of trust and faith in large institutions and "experts." Just 2% of American children are being home schooled and 1% are enrolled in charter schools, but the numbers belie the impact these alternative learning environments are having on K-12 education and society at large. Home schools are legal in every state but are generally unregulated, with parents or other adults using the abundant instructional resources that can be accessed. Churches provide lesson plans to the roughly one-half of home schoolers who are religiously motivated (evolution is the big bang of reasons fundamentalists take their kids out of public school). Others feel public schools don't provide a very good education, are unsafe, or are just not right for their child. The smaller student-to-teacher ratio and parents' personal involvement in their children's education are advantages difficult to argue with. Many home schoolers also take advantage of certain resources of public schools where allowed, sending their kids to art and music classes and sports activities. Although many believe home schoolers to be an army of Pugsleys and Wednesdays, it's simply not true. They are for the most part very normal and self-directed kids who, in fact, often win the national Spelling Bee, score higher than average on SATs, and nab the occasional Rhodes scholarship. Charter schools are a much different beast, publicly-funded, tuition-free institutions that subscribe to a particular philosophy of education. Around for the last decade, charter schools receive about $5,000 per student from their state's coffers, making them potentially for-profit organizations. With that kind of carrot dangling, it's not too surprising that there's been some funny business going on, ranging from phantom students to the teaching of religion, which is illegal. The latest development is, what else, online charter schools where students learn readin', ritin', and 'rithmetic over the Internet and communicate with their teachers by phone, e-mail, and chat rooms. Home and charter schools are islands of independence, the little red schoolhouses of the 21st century. Take a lesson from this very American idea of going one's own way when moral issues are at stake.

Offer liberty to consumers disenchanted with the status quo in your product category.

WORK : Soloists

As Corporate America continues to get as svelte as Jared from Subway fame, more workers are finding themselves members of a growing freelance (and e-lance) nation. Others are choosing to be outsourced, farmed out, and otherwise occupationally unfettered and fancy free, attracted by the freedom and flexibility that life on the outside of the company town affords. Emerging out of the rubble of the traditional concept of work, where employer and employee were once in it together, is a new paradigm of work based on the concept of independent "soloists." Soloists work for themselves, sometimes as wandering global nomads who apply their expertise on a particular project and then move on to the next gig. Many museums, for example, hurt by budget cutbacks, are now hiring independent art curators to produce shows. Besides saving money on staff salaries, museums get to pick and choose experts who are worldwide authorities in their particular field. Journeymen like Hon Henru, who hails from China, lives in Paris, and recently advised a museum in Amsterdam, or Okwui Enwezor, originally from Nigeria, based in New York, and curator of show in Germany, represent this new wave of peripatetic job floater. An additional benefit is a cross-pollination of ideas as independents blow some fresh air into sometimes musty museum atmospheres. Way on the other side of the work fence, the information technology sector too is adopting a soloist model, more often relying on displaced techies who've had their Internet bubble popped. InfoBridge, a Chicago-area company, estimates that the number of freelance IT pros jumped from 10% to 30% from 1999 to 2001, and places some 300 consultants wherever the geeky action is around the world. In response to the millions of workers who are flying solo by choice or out of necessity, a number of websites are online to get employers and employees together. Sites such as InstantWork.com, The CentralMall.com, Elance.com, SoloGig.com, and CreativeMoonlighter.com are matchmakers of the working universe, allowing companies and individuals to find each other and see if something double-clicks. Soloists typically fill out job profiles and post their credentials, while clients scan candidates and contact them if there seems to be a fit for a particular project. Through such services, soloists in web design, writing, marketing, education/training, travel/ tourism, and photography/illustration get to cruise the global job market without either party having to commit to a full-time position. As the days of retiring with the gold watch become an even more distant memory, prepare yourself for lots more occupations to go solo.

Orchestrate your marketing plans based on a global economy buzzing with independent worker bees.

FILM :
Indie Film

A generation ago, everyone and his brother wanted to write the Great American Novel. Today it's all about independent film, especially for 20-somethings and 30-somethings who were raised on MTV and are hard-wired to think visually. For rebels with a camera who want to steer clear from the tyranny of Hollywood, indie film is *the* way to express oneself. Fortunately for them, the galaxy of indie film is expanding like a supernova, as more of us look for movies that have not rolled off the Hollywood assembly line. Film Movement, a new start-up, for example, sends first-run indie film DVDs every month to subscribers for $189 a year. The number of independent film festivals too continues to grow, opportunities to see some great movies, show one's work, meet distributors, and simply celebrate one's cinematic freedom. Ever since the Sundance Film Festival got a little too mainstream for its own good, real Indies have headed to Slamdance in Park City, Utah. The names of other independent film festivals—the IFP/Midwest Flyover Zone Short Film Festival in Chicago, the Kudzu Film Festival in Athens, Georgia, and Flickapalooza in Los Angeles, to name just a few—make it perfectly clear that this subculture walks to the beat of a different drummer. Cable television is another prime outlet to exhibit and see indie films, ranging from the big-time (the Independent Film Channel) to local stations offering free access. Not surprisingly, independent filmmakers have glommed onto the most indie of media—the Internet—and, in the process, have begun to revolutionize the movie business. Sites such as IndieUnderground.com provide an alternative distribution system for the cream of the indie crop, a virtual, international storefront that is always open for business. Digital video bypasses the evil empire of the "Industry," offering epic savings in overhead and distribution costs and the possibility for an independent filmmaker to actually make a profit. More and more projects are indeed being shot on digital video, then edited on desktop computers, and finally streamed via satellite over the Internet. As broadband comes online, this democratization of the filmmaking and distribution process will become even greater, furthering a shift in power from the moguls to the artists. Working its magic on the edges of our most identifiable of art forms, indie film is a trend begging to be leveraged in other product categories.

Declare your independence from the mainstream pack by developing "indie" products and services that defy the status quo.

MUSIC : Indie Labels

"Think like an independent, act like a major."
—Jordan Schur, owner/founder of Flip Records

They read like a who's who of the darker side: Napalm; Relapse; Vagrant; Anti; Screaming Ferret Wreckords. Indie music labels boil and bubble, toil and trouble on the perimeter of the record business, surviving by targeting niche and underground audiences the major labels are not very good reaching. Compared to risk-phobic majors which shoot for gold and platinum (a million plus units), sales of indies typically number in the thousands, rounding error for entertainment conglomerates. Whether specializing in sub-genres like Goth Metal or "emo" (a fusion of punk and intensely emotional, there's-an-ache-in-my-heart rock) or else shotgunning across genres, indie labels know their audience. By focusing on a limited number of artists and bands, launching grassroots campaigns involving guerilla-style street teams, and following the three rules of the music biz (tour, tour, tour), indie labels have a chance of slinging a rock into the eyes of a major Goliath. National retain chains are also geared for multimillion sales, so indie labels typically rely on indie stores to deliver the goods and align themselves with majors on the distribution end.

But with the mainstream record business currently as limp as a bizkit or creamed korn, there's a window of opportunity for indie labels to get a piece of humble pie and realize under-the-radar profitability. Indies have always fed major labels with innovative artists, bands, and entire genres, a classic study of how the once fringe (e.g., hip-hop or Seattle grunge) becomes trendy becomes mainstream and then mutates into something else. By allowing acts to stay true to their artistic vision ("keep it real"), and by cultivating their careers over time, indie labels contrast with the in-and-out, make-it-or-break-it philosophy of the majors. Some artists like Paul Westerberg or Tom Waits prefer this TLC over TRL, opting for more control over their musical destiny rather than a greater chance of fame and fortune. Major labels routinely scoop up promising indie acts (such as R.E.M., Green Day, or, more recently, the red hot White Stripes who moved from Sympathy to V2, a subsidiary of Virgin), but often water the original soup down until it no longer smells like teenage spirit. Listen up to indie music and to those who don't want their MTV.

Think like an independent, act like a major in your category as a best-of-both-worlds marketing strategy.

FASHION : Alternative Jeans

"Diesel cannot be held responsible for any out of body experiences, violent acts of nature, unexpected delusions of grandeur, sporadic demonstrations of passion or similar occurrences while wearing our product."
—Diesel Bureau for International Communication

It used to pretty simple when it came to buying jeans. You'd go out and get another pair of Levi's, possibly Lee's, when your favorite pair shredded somewhere between the wash and rinse cycle. The rare exceptions to this rule were if you were going to go to or be in a rodeo, in which you'd get a pair of Wrangler's, or if you were going to a disco, in which you'd buy brands of jeans let's just agree not to talk about. That has, of course, all changed. Much of the original color of Levi's, which patented riveted "waist overalls" in 1873, has bled, the company caught with its pants down when competitors altered the orbit of the jeans galaxy. Today we're living in a decidedly blue period as a number of azure upstarts saturate the category with new styles and compelling brand presences. Nothing is coming between teens and $100+ jeans with studded seams, embroidered hems, and beaded waistbands, and retailer American Eagle now offers "customization stations" to stencil, razor, or pumice that pair of mood indigos. Mudd is the biggest thing to splash the teenage girls market since the Spice Girls, offering moderately priced jeans that are turning Generation Y into Generation Mariah. With its Lace-Ups with frayed hems and side seams, hip-huggin' Brazilian-cut Ipanemas, groovy High Break Bells, and Acid Washes with the super-limbo rise, Mudd had made jeans fun and daring again. Their psychedelic website even lets you "Ask the Jeans Genie" any question relating or not relating to denim. Diesel too is energizing the category not only with styles like its Super Stripes but with innovative promotions designed, in the Italian company's satirical yet somehow genuine words, "for successful living." In addition to their Diesel-U-Music website feature showcasing the best in UK underground music, the company sponsors an international fashion competition and a series of 96 books created by contributing artists. Other brands like LEI (Life-Energy-Intelligence), Seven, Mavi, and Miss Sixty are also bringing revolution to the jeans streets, turning a quintessential American icon (the average guy or gal owns seven pairs) into a dizzy array of red, white, and, of course, blue. The jeans business is a colorful case study of the splintering of consumer culture, reminding us that marketing, like the universe itself, is constantly expanding and morphing. Constantly reinvent your category or face the prospect of fading away.

Make every day Independence Day with products and services that run against the stream.

SHOPPING: Indie Retail

After about a half century, it appears that the clone-it-and-they-will-come model of retailing may be finally over. The DNA of large chains and franchises—uniformity, consistency, no surprises—is gradually breaking down as consumers exhibit a different genetic profile when shopping and take their money elsewhere. From the redwood forest to the gulfstream waters, many retailers are proving that this indie land was made for you and me. In New York, for example, Dylan's Candy Bar is a monument to glucose, thinking outside the box of chocolates with more than 5,000 types of candy. Also in the city so nice they named it twice, the Strand Bookstore is proving you don't need to cappuccino, mochaccino, or frappaccino readers to sell books. A fiercely independent family business, the Strand is five floors of literary goodness, offering not only the standard fare but also hard-to-find books your big-box bookstore remaindered long ago. Head down Broadway a mile or so and scurry over to Yellow Rat Bastard, perhaps the world capital of alternative retail. The store is an indie brandathon, equipping homeys and chicks with alt-gear from Caffeine, UFO, Lithium, Madsoul, and, of course, Porn Star and Pimp Gear. Subscribe to their in-house magazine, *YRB*, to get the dope on music, street culture, and arts and photography. Across the Hudson, indie retail is alive and well in places like Durham, North Carolina, whose Ninth Street is an avenue of freedom for shoppers in the Research Triangle. The McDonalds there is not the eponymous hamburger chain but rather an indie café complete with soda jerk (that would be Mrs. McDonald). In Ft. Lauderdale, shoppers deserving a break today are getting up and getting away to Las Olas Boulevard, a tree-lined promenade where window shopping is not déjà vu all over again. This boulevard of dreams has about 100 small shops and galleries including Cheeburger, Cheeburger (I have a hunch they serve Pepsi there), Joe Picasso Clay Studio (a blend of java and pottery painting), and Just Africa (*the* place in South Florida to get that carved Pygmy bed). By carrying unique products and offering personal service, locally-based, entrepreneurial merchants in urban villages like Thornton Park Central in downtown Orlando are attracting and keeping a loyal clientele, serving up a minty fresh alternative to the plain vanilla suburban mall. And in the nation's Cheese Belt, stores such as Twinkle, Twinkle Children's Boutique in Shawano and the Munchkin Boutique in Neenah are giving Wisconsinites choice in kids' clothing, selling brands that can't be found at national chains. Expect "e pluribus consumerism" ("diversity in shopping") to become retailers' rallying cry.

Colonize indie thinking as more consumers sail away from the chains of the Old World.

HOSPITALITY: Boutique Hotels

You're on the road again and you wake up in the middle of the night. Where in the world are you? Oh yeah, Atlanta. You know, you think to yourself, this hotel room looks just like last week's in Houston. And the one in Detroit the week before that. And the one in Kansas City the week before that. And the one...This Kafkaesque nightmare is less likely to become reality as more boutique hotels offer travelers an alternative to generic chains that have the personality of beige carpet. A handful of independent hotel groups are just saying no to business as usual, bringing aesthetics, intimacy, and one-of-a-kindness to the hospitality party. After a post 9/11 dip in bookings, boutique hotels are back on track, injecting brand identity into a largely commodified category. The king of boutique hotels, Ian Schrager, set the standard with the Delano in South Beach, but others are determined to rule the indie roost. Kimpton is keeping the away-from-home fires burning with its strategy of renovating and repositioning old buildings into charming hotels designed to look and feel like a guest room in a friend's home. Next time you're in San Francisco, consider staying at Kimpton's Hotel Triton where you can rent a room designed by Jerry Garcia or the "Black Magic Bedroom" inspired by another Bay Area rock star, Carlos Santana. You're likely to find a tarot card reader or DJ spinning disks in the lobby or in the hotel's "Zen Den."

If classical music is more your druthers, consider the Joie De Vivre group's Archbishop's Mansion at Alamo Square, a French-style chateau with each room named after a different opera. Even stodgy Washington, DC and Boston have boarded the boutique bus, with hotels like Rouge and Topaz taking some of the stuffiness out of our capital city and Destination Hotel's Nine Zero baking in Beantown. The names of Nine Zero's meeting rooms—Create, Reflect, Imagine—alone speak to the emergence of a new paradigm of hospitality that has a sense of soulfulness and even wellness. Not surprisingly, traditional chains like Starwood Resorts and Marriott's Renaissance brand are easing down the boutique road (also attracted to the fact that the average cost of developing a room in a boutique hotel is less than half that in a new chain). Starwood's W Hotels are a brilliant blend of high-tech (high-speed Internet access and CD/video libraries) and high-touch (fresh apples, juice bars, pet-friendly policies, and Aveda bath products), providing an oxymoronic oasis of connectivity. Expect others in travel and hospitality to secede from the union of boringness.

Open up a boutique philosophy in your business to make an emotional connection with consumers.

TRANSPORTATION : Private Jets

Who would not want to declare independence from today's less-than-friendly skies? Private jets are soaring, a trend that was already accelerating before 9/11 but became turbo-charged when safety concerns and airport delays intensified. Despite the tight economy, more and more people are saying that private jets are the only way to fly, and we're not just talking about rock stars, leggy supermodels, and Thurston Howell IIIs. In big-bucks deals where teleconferences and Webcasts just won't do, private jets allow executives to jump on a plane with just a few hours notice, saving time, energy, and sometimes, even money. Private jets make the most sense for shorter hops, for larger groups, and for less traveled routes which commercial airliners don't serve very well or not at all. Private jets can land in some 5,000 airports in the USA (including take-me-away places like Martha's Vineyard and Sun Valley), ten times the number of bigger birds. Rather than owning one's own private jet, whose upkeep and maintenance are even more than that of a horse, many are opting for fractional interests or ownerships that are the aeronautic equivalent to a time-share condominium. Sign a lease based on your estimated usage and before you can say up, up, and away, you're sitting in a Gulfstream or Learjet that makes commercial first class seem like the back of the bus. Fractional interests have experienced 38% annual growth since 1995, according to Bombardier Flexjet of Dallas, a leader in the field. The National Business Airline Association says there are about 3,500 fractional owners, a number growing every year as more executives ask for it as part of their compensation package. An added bonus of private jets is their superior safety (triple-redundancy in technical systems versus double in commercial planes) and personnel who, oddly enough, actually seem like they don't hate their jobs and people in general. Highly-trained and extremely well-screened staffs are on board to make jetsetters' flights as safe as possible and offer full concierge services, more than enough reason for many to get on board. Count on more privatized services to effectively compete with public ones when time and convenience are at stake.

Cater to consumers' schedules versus yours to lift yourself above the competition.

FOOD & BEVERAGE : Artisan Foods

If the 19th and 20th centuries were about any one thing, they were arguably about the remarkable ability we developed to make things exactly alike through machines. The corollary of mass production is, as any Marxist can and will tell you, mass consumption, the vicious circle which keeps the wheels of consumer capitalism humming like those on an any-color-as-long-as-it's-black Model-T. The 21st century, however, is in some ways turning out to be more like the 13th and 14th centuries, when artisans served up handcrafted foods to ye olde target markets in Europe. Independent artisan cheese makers like Carr Valley Cheese of Wisconsin have revived the craft, creating "monastery-like" blends of cow, goat, and sheep milk that have consumers mooing for more. Using only "farmstead" milk (produced only on the farm), boutique cheese makers churn out varieties that distant cousin Velveeta wouldn't even recognize as kin. Zingerman's Creamery in Manchester, Michigan makes small batches of cream cheese by hand which is so yummy you won't mind forking over the $10 per pound. Restaurants like New York's Artisanal are also offering flights of artsy cheeses, with fromageriers watching over their tilsits, rustic blues, pepatos, and telemes like a mother hen over her chicks. Other purveyors of cholesterol are producing artisan bacon—thick, organic, and smoky slabs of porcine goodness that make Oscar Meyer seem like a wienie. Companies like Carlton's and Nueske's feed their little piggies a special diet of organic grains, making them better fed than Krispy Kremed humans. Join The Grateful Palate's Bacon-of-the-Month Club and you'll be in hog heaven, squealing in delight from their slow-cured, hand-seasoned pork bellies. Artisan bread too is popping up fresh across the country, giving consumers handmade lovin' from the oven. Panera Bread is well on the way to becoming the upper crust of the bread world, offering a high-quality yet still affordable alternative to fast food. Indies like Artisan Bakers in Sonoma make bread, cookies, pastries, and desserts from scratch and use local ingredients whenever possible. Oil, vinegar, and honey have also gone the artisan route as small exporters turn basic commodities into extraordinary specialty foods. Whether 10 year old Trebbiano balsamic vinegar aged in 300 year old barrels, cold pressed extra virgin olive oil from ancient Florentine trees, or organic lemon blossom honey made by nomadic beekeepers on the north coast of Sicily, artisan foods are nibbling away at the middle of the mainstream plate. Keep your eyes peeled as this pre-industrial revolution picks up more steam.

Be the artisan of your category and satisfy consumers' taste for handcrafted products.

TREND COMMANDMENT 3
Declare Independence.

KA-CHING!

AUTOS
Head to Independence Boulevard to break away from the every-car-looks-alike pack.

BEAUTY
Apply the in-your-face attitude of indie music and indie fashion to create an "alt-beauty" segment.

ENTERTAINMENT & MEDIA
Widen the lens of indie film to build an indie media empire.

FASHION
Knock off the energy fueling alternative jeans to supercharge your brands.

FINANCIAL
Plant your flag in investment alternatives to follow-the-sheep mutual funds.

FOOD & BEVERAGE

Can quantity and accent quality in your marketing recipe to declare independence from me-too competitors.

HEALTHCARE

Develop products and services that bypass today's ailing healthcare system.

RETAIL

Take stock in yourself by making your stores different from all others.

TECHNOLOGY

Define your mission as to allow consumers to be more self-sufficient through technology.

TRAVEL & HOSPITALITY

Take travelers down the road less traveled.

4

TREND COMMANDMENT

Deliver Experience.

TREND COMMANDMENT 4
Deliver Experience.

In our land of organic milk and honey, many of us have visited much of materialism and brought home the t-shirt. In less oblique terms, much of our acquisitional or possessive needs have been met in our society of middle class abundance, pushing us up Maslow's hierarchy towards the promised land of self-actualization. The result has been a wholesale shift in the weighty concepts of identity and status, changing our individual and collective orientation from materialism towards experience. Many of us are investing in our "experiential portfolio," the memory-based credits we deposit in the account of accounts, our lives. Although money will always make the world go around, one might think about a different form of currency in circulation which, after some accumulation, adds up to experiential wealth, an alternative or complement to financial wealth. Trying new things, learning new stuff, achieving new goals, and feeling new sensations are all means to earn experiential wealth, none of which shows up on a balance sheet or income statement. Whether physical, emotional, spiritual, intellectual, sensual, or virtual, experiences are intangible but fixed assets that can't break or wear out. You can't lose half of your experiences in a divorce. And unlike possessions, which are symbolic and reflect who we are, experiences are actual and *are* who we are. Things, in other words, are external and express our identity while experiences are internal and make up our identity.

This distinction may seem rhetorical but is crucial for those in business who, when you think about it for a second, sell either things (products) or experiences (services). All marketers have to shift from a passive voice to an active one, and translate their products' reason-for-being into experiential terms. Think of consumers as anthropomorphic sharks constantly feeding on new experiences to gobble up and digest. At the end of the day, many are realizing, it is what you've done versus what you've owned that really matters, that we are on Earth not to wear a pair of Jimmy Choos or a Rolex Oyster Perpetual but to experience as much of life as we can or want to. Baby boomers especially are wanting to seize the experiential day, knowing now it is not the one with the most toys who wins but rather the one who has achieved what he or she wanted to achieve. Here are a few trends that should help you think of some experiences to deliver to consumers' doors.

EDUCATION: Internships

Remember the good old days when students spent most of their time in school? These days, the lines between education and work are getting mighty fuzzy as more students take internships during what is now often called their "academic career." Both high schoolers and college students are pursuing "experiential learning," using internships to get on the fast track to success. 77% of American college seniors have interned by the time they graduate, according to Vault Inc., with 66% having served two internships. Why the urgency to get out of the ivory tower and into the real world, especially when most internships are unpaid and do not offer college credit? Internships are ideal resume fodder, clear proof to potential future employers that one has got his or her career feet wet. Some employers in fact consider internships to be a prerequisite for new hirers, a prime way to screen candidates in today's tough job climate. Jobs do indeed result from the contacts one makes while interning, with 57% of interns getting offers for full-time positions by their sponsors, according to the National Association of Colleges and Employers. But interning is much more than turbocharging one's C.V., also used by students to dip their toes into a particular field before diving in head first. Students find out what they like to do and, even more important, what they don't like to do, learning things not taught at Harvard

Business School or anywhere else. More than 2,000 students from across the country take internships in D.C. each year arranged through the Washington Center, a nonprofit which places college students anywhere from the Sierra Club to the Girl Scouts of America. Internship fever has trickled down to the high school level, a side effect being that teenage employment levels are currently at record lows. Teens know that an internship at a hospital, radio station, senator's office, law firm, or museum is going to score a lot more points with an Ivy League admissions officer than having been named "Employee of the Week" at Arby's. Every summer, teens from wealthy families flock to New York to take internships in fashion, music, publishing, and film to merge into the fast lane, their living expenses underwritten by Mummy and Daddy. Here too, however, interning is more than just getting named "Most Likely to Succeed." Internships bring education to life and serve as an opportunity to solve problems in the workplace in a supportive environment. Look for internships to continue to be seen as an experiential bridge between students and the greater community and as a wise investment for those who can afford them.

Create products and services for consumers who know there's no substitute for experience.

HEALTHCARE :
Massage Therapy

The Chinese and Indians knew it 3,000 years ago. So did the ancient Romans and Greeks. Massage therapy is a sensory experience with abundant healing powers, rubbing more of us the right way. All of our senses are constantly bombarded with stimuli except, strangely, touch, which is no doubt driving many of us to seek out the nurturing experience of having another person's hands on our body. The number of Americans who visited a massage therapist doubled between 1997 and 2002, according to the American Massage Therapist Association, with 17% of us getting over 100 million massages a year. Massage therapy is now a $5-billion-a-year business, with about 200,000 therapists pressing the flesh at $45-$80 an hourly pop. Why the growing need to get kneaded? Massage therapy is at the healthy heart of holistic (mind-body-spirit) wellness, delivering both emotional and physical benefits. Some researchers say that up to 80% of diseases are somehow stress-related, justification enough for many to consider massage therapy an untouchable affordable indulgence. Hard data is helping massage walk the walk and talk the talk, its therapeutic effects including improved circulation, which gets more oxygen into the blood and more toxins out. With a reduced heart rate, lower blood pressure, and boosted immune system, it's no wonder one feels calmer and less anxious after getting poked, prodded, and pampered. Corporate America is flexing its muscle with massage therapy, as companies like G.E., Goldman Sachs,

Young & Rubicam, Motorola, and American Airlines offer it as an on-site, morale-boosting, productivity-enhancing perk. Hospitals too are giving out free touchie-feelies, part of their gradual transformation into wellness centers combining the best of Western medicine and Eastern homeopathy. (The number of hospitals offering alternative therapies has nearly doubled from 1998 according to the American Hospital Association, and 78% of the nation's 125 medical schools—including Harvard, Yale, Stanford, Georgetown, and Johns Hopkins—now teach courses in alternative care.) More HMOs and insurance companies are picking up the tab for massage as its pain-reducing benefits are proven in research studies. And with massage therapy known to raise the level of good-guy brain chemicals like serotonin and dopamine and reduce stress-causing blue meanies like cortisol, it's not surprising to find more massage therapists at airports. The Massage Bar at the Seattle-Tacoma airport and Nashville International and the Massage Garage at Calgary International are just two firms to see massages fly through the roof after 9/11. Whether it's slow and steady Deep Tissue, extremity-based Reflexology, energy-flowing Shiatsu, kinky four-handed, leave-your-clothes-on Aquamassage, or good old Swedish, massage therapy has the pulse on sensory experience.

Squeeze some stress-reducing products or services into your marketing plans.

SHOPPING:
DIY Retail

Been there, bought that. Some retailers are realizing that there is a whole other level of shopping that elevates it from a purely consumptive experience to a participatory, productive one. More do-it-yourself retail is headed to your town, appealing to consumers who want to be an actor on the shopping stage. Pottery painting stores, which bubbled up in the mid-90s, continue to shake and bake, turning ordinary folks into accomplished artists. Kids and adults choose an unfinished piece of pottery, design and decorate it as they wish, and return in a few days to find it glazed, fired, and microwave-friendly. Most stores, like Our Name is Mud in New York, As You Wish in Phoenix, and the Pottery Bayou in the Chicago 'burbs make pottery painting the centerpiece of a birthday party, bridal shower, or baby shower. The Pottery Bayou also offers "Art Adventure Camps," throwing smocks on kids who turn out flower pots and heirloom cookie jars complete with their own handprints. Pothead, also on the outskirts of the city with big shoulders, caters to the corporate crowd, claiming that pot parties at their place or yours motivate employees and build confidence. Other DIY retail concepts are smoking, particularly Build-A-

Bear workshop. With over a hundred stores and still growing, Build-A-Bear is becoming a grizzly of the retail woods by delivering a fun and memorable family shopping experience rather than just another thing to buy. Bear builders create a stuffed teddy from scratch, choosing a shell style, degree of "plushiness," and its contents. All bears come with a heart (a wise move considering the trials and tribulations that faced the coronary-challenged Tin Man), but clothing (e.g., undergarments, two-piece bikinis, hospital scrubs, surfer sandals) and accessories (e.g., boxing gloves) are extra, as are audio messages (e.g., "Will you marry me?"). Build-A-Bear won the National Retail Federation's International Innovator of the Year award in 2001, a clear sign that they are onto something big. Watch the fur fly in DIY retail as others turn shopping into a warm and fuzzy experience.

Build DIY into your workshop through products and services that let consumers experience the creative process.

SOCIALIZING:
Theme Parties

Now's your chance to get your childhood or that train wreck you remember as your teenage years right. More adults are throwing theme parties steeped in yesterday, enjoying events and get-togethers which poke gentle fun at while also pay tribute to seminal experiences of youth. Slumber parties, for example, are quite the rage, as everyday chicks and glitterati like Oprah and Bianca grab their blankees for a sleepover. Pajama games are held at either a hotel or somebody's home, with manicures, pedicures, junk food, and drinks (no, not chocolate milk or juice boxes) standard fare. As in grade school, slumbering is actually the least of it, with friends staying up really, really late to giggle about who's not there. Fast forward a decade or so to prom night, another activity otherwise normal adults are choosing to experience once again. Mid-life prom goers rent out a gym or hotel ballroom, dig out that tux with the ruffled shirt or insert-color-not-found-in-nature-here dress (or buy one at Buy-Prom-Dress.com) and party like its 1979. Don't forget the cummerbund, boys, or, for that matter, the Flock of Seagulls haircut. The faux ivy arch is a must for an updated photographic keepsake, with extra credit for crepe paper streamers or a disco ball. Head up into your attic to find that mixed cassette you made for the pre-party kegger (you know, the one with Pure Prairie League's "Amy" on it) and, needless to say, it's strictly BYOF (Bring Your Own Flask). Last but not least, remember to get lucky in the back seat of a K-car, worrying all the time that a deranged psychopath will at any moment approach your vehicle and kill you dead with a steak knife. Sounds a might loony, but theme parties like prom nights (as well as bar mitzvahs, regardless of one's religious reference) are the stuff of many post-post-pubescents' dreams, especially in the fantasy capital of the world, Los Angeles. Such experiences reflect baby boomers' intent to not only look young (can you say, "Botox"?) but act young, and represent a last chance to relive childhood before it returns completely irony-free as a geezer. Brace yourself as the generation that refuses to completely grow up saves the last dance for themselves in more ways.

Celebrate good times (c'mon!) by repackaging experiences linked to consumer's youth.

ENTERTAINMENT :
Digital Gaming

Americans got game, and I'm not just talking about trigger-happy geeks and get-a-life social misfits. 145 million of us (that's 60%) play video games, according to a recent survey by the Interactive Digital Software Association, with North American sales of games and related hardware adding up to $11.7 billion in 2002. That's more than total annual movie ticket sales but, with 25% growth a year, the games have just begun. Digital gaming is already the fastest growing segment of the entertainment industry, suggesting that it may very well turn out to be in the 21st century what movies were in the 20th. For those of you who wouldn't know Super Mario from Crash Bandicoot, digital gaming is played on video game systems (SONY's PlayStation 2, Nintendo's GameCube or handheld GameBoy, Microsoft's XBOX), online (XBOX Live, RealNetwork's subscription model, Yahoo!'s fee-based system), or on PCs. Experience is digital gaming's middle name, made possible by interactive software so graphically rich that if Da Vinci or Michaelangelo were alive today, they'd probably be video game designers creating splatterfests of color and sound. In the classic, narrative-driven RPG (Role Playing Game) format, players exist in the first person, the protagonist in a supernatural or paranormal story highly (and hopefully) unlikely to unfold in real life. Some games allow players to customize their skin color and gender (choose from male, female, alien, or bot) and select a set of skills or special powers, creating an entire life story in the process. Players then typically embark on a quest of epic proportions, exploring alternative universes and other worlds to fight evil, overcome obstacles, or solve puzzles. The deliverables are action, adventure, escape, and fun, simultaneously real and surreal as players enter multi-level, non-linear, hyper-aware, and adrenaline-rushing sensory environments. Time and space as we know them do not apply, as titles like Bioware's "Knights of the Old Republic," Gray Matter's "Redneck Rampage," Monkeystone Games's "Hyperspace Delivery Boy," or Sega's "Jet Set Radio Future" suggest. It is Rockstar Games's series of "Grand Theft Auto," however, which has all gamers trash talking, allowing players' alter egos to steal cars, pick up hookers, and beat up the occasional pedestrian. Quaking a little in their boots and perhaps worried that their own businesses may be doomed, entertainment and other marketers are partnering with game boys big time. With little ninjas now playing video games in the backseat of cars and as broadband, wireless, and artificial intelligence come on board, the possibilities are virtually infinite. Hope you're game as the electronic arts become an odyssey of experience.

Create products and service that allow consumers' identities to morph and mutate.

ONLINE:
Webcasting

Remember that Victoria Secret runway webcast back in '99 that got more hits than Cheech and Chong in the 1970s? Webcasting soon went bust but is perky once again, increasingly used to reach more narrowly defined audiences. As multimedia, virtual experiences, webcasts are bringing a host of events and information to people all around the world, often in real time. The funeral industry, for example, is gradually integrating webcasting into their services, beaming electronic eulogies to relatives and buddies who could not attend the service in person. Funeral home webmasters digitally record a service, upload it onto their site and, before you can say ashes to ashes, dust to dust, cousin Ernie in Auckland is shedding a virtual tear. The White House has realized the digital photo op potential of webcasting, streaming the last Easter Egg Roll live followed by the First Lady reading a book to children on the South Lawn. Entertainment and sports marketers too are delivering their products online to folks who can't make it to the show or game but have RealPlayer, Windows MediaPlayer, Apple QuickTime, or another streaming audio player on their computers. Over HOB.com, for example, the House of Blues has cybercast hundreds of concerts held at their various venues, giving listeners and viewers the chance to hear and see everyone from A Tribe Called Quest to Zap Mama. Webcasts of major league, minor league, and college sports too can be readily found online (now more often for a fee), allowing all of us to keep up with the current goings-on in Australian rules football and cricket. Check out Syracuse.com or OregonLive.com, for example, to listen to the respective minor league baseball games of the Skychiefs and Beavers. Radio websites which broadcast exclusively over the Internet, such as KPIG.com, offer listeners the chance to hear music that is way beyond the range of local stations, and often in near CD-quality. Academia too is rah-rah on webcasting, as universities and associations archive lectures and conference presentations for virtual smarty-pants (go to ChronicleofHigherEducation.com for a brainy taste). Best of all, many webcasts are interactive, allowing sender and sendee to engage in a real-time Q&A. Insomniacs may want to visit ABC.com to chat it up with the anchors of "ABC World News Now" at 2 a.m. EST. Many businesses are also webcasting, using it for CEO pep talks, sales training, marketing launches, client meetings, internal communications, and financial updates to the investor community. As compression technologies turn webcasting into the next (and cheaper) generation of video conferencing and satellite broadcasting, get ready to finally experience Edward R. Murrow's 50 year-old declaration, "You Are There."

Create experiential, interactive relationships with consumers through your marketing web.

TRAVEL:
Adventure Travel

"The destination has become incidental to the experience."
—Peter Greenberg, author of The Travel Detective

How better to make a deposit in one's experiential portfolio than by investing some (ad)venture capital? Adventure travel is a segment industry not held hostage to terrorism or even the rocky economy, as have-backpack-will-travels trek the Inca Trail in Machu Picchu, go on safari in Kenya, retrace Darwin's steps in the Galapagos Islands, or follow Ernest Shakleton's route through Antarctica. One of the bigger dogs in adventure travel is dog sledding, with outfitters from New Hampshire to Alaska ready to turn one's call of the wild into mush. At Voyager's Outward Bound North Woods Expeditions in northern Minnesota or Idida Ride (get it?) Sled Dog Tours in Seward, Alaska, for example, white fangs are experiencing truly dog day afternoons. Mushers lead their six-dog team of Huskies, Alaskan Malamutes, and Samoyeds through snowy woods and across frozen lakes, learning how to make these born-to-runs go ("Hike!"), turn right ("Gee!"), turn left ("Haw!"), go straight ("On by!"), and stop ("Whoa!"). Learning the obvious advantage of being the lead dog and not to put yourself in the middle of a dogfight are two pieces of wisdom worth taking home. For an adventure of an entirely different breed, consider IslandQuest's "Survivor Vacation" in St. Croix in the US Virgin Islands.

Inspired by the TV show, teams compete against each other by racing kayaks, snorkeling for treasure, and climbing ropes, with the winner taking home up to $7,000. No eating of bugs required, and you can't be voted off the island. Those wanting to tie ropes instead of climb them are saddling over to Cowgirl Camp at the Lazy K Bar, a 23-room guest ranch on 160 acres in the Tucson Mountains. Ladies learn how to round up cattle while riding a horse, with an all-girl rodeo the climax of the long weekend. Yee-haw! Finally, for those in pursuit of an experiential meltdown, the Chernobyl Tour in the Ukraine awaits. Sixteen years after the worst nuclear disaster in history, Kiev StarTours is leading minibus tours of the trashed reactor and the deserted town of Pripyat (personal radiation monitors provided). Watch adventure travel take off as we seek out experiences that make us glow with pride and satisfaction.

Put adventure at the core of your brand's reason-for-being.

Food & Beverage:
Gourmet Retreats

Find the Iron Chef a little too...grating? You may be ripe for a gourmet retreat. Gourmet retreats are culinary adventures offering visitors a kind of gastronomic experience that can't be beat, whipped, or frappéd. Leading gourmet retreats include Ballymaloe ("good food") Cookery School in County Cork, Ireland, where the lucky and charmed have been going since 1983 to squash the idea that Irish cooking is about boiling tubers and cabbage. Guests from around the world take classes and watch demonstrations, learning everything from how to make one's next Christmas a magical feast to how to forage for food in the lush, rolling countryside. For just as long, folks have headed down under to the Howqua Dale Residential Cooking School for a hands-on, participative immersion in Australian cuisine. Guests gather in the school's "fish-bowl in a paddock" kitchen and come away with the ability to do much more than throw another shrimp on the barbie. Closer to home, La Varenne at the Greenbrier in White Sulpher Springs, West Virginia offers a 5-day cooking program every spring in a poshier than posh atmosphere. And at CasaLana, a gourmet retreat located in Calistoga in the Napa Valley, diehard foodies learn how to slice, dice, and rice from some of California's best chefs. Enrollment is limited to 8-12 people per class, and students receive recipe hand-outs and a generous helping of the eats cooked up. State-of-the-art kitchens, equipment, tools, and knives are provided, so all visitors have to bring is their appetite for experience. CasaLana also mixes it up by taking guests on excursions to specialty and ethnic food markets, farmers' markets, winemakers, and growers to learn about food at or closer to its source. At virtually all gourmet retreats, the emphasis is on using ingredients that are in season and on how to pair food with wine, skills that separate the pit bulls from the poodles in the dog-eat-dog world of high-end cooking. Gourmet retreats are all about experience, offering consumers a way of improving one's chops in one of life's tastier arenas.

Sprinkle experience liberally throughout your marketing plans to turn up your brands' heat.

TOURISM:
Heritage Tourism

Better watch your backs, Mickey and Donald, heritage tourism is nipping at your heels. Heritage tourism—traveling to places indigenous to a particular people and their culture —is now one of the top five vacation activities, according to the Travel Industry Association of America. Heritage tourism explores the real life stories of the past and present, its rising popularity a backlash perhaps against the Great American Vacation oriented around a mythological menagerie of mice and ducks. Some wiser state tourism boards are reading the experiential handwriting on the wall, marketing what I call "reality travel" as an alternative to escapist fantasy. Virginia, for example, is promoting 100 sites and attractions related to African American heritage and culture, including churches, cemeteries, museums, monuments, and schools. But it is, interestingly, Native Americans who have their ears closest to the ground in tourism. Rather than go to Frontierland again, they're asking, why wouldn't tourists prefer to go to what was not that long ago the real frontier? Various Indian tribes are serving as hosts to the adventurous and curious from the four corners of the Earth, showing them first-hand what life was like for native populations before tourists of a couple centuries back decided to stay for awhile. For example, with their Lodgepole Gallery and Tipi Village near Browning, Montana, the Blackfeet are putting up tenderfeet in tipis which are authentic as any, save the foam mattress on the ground. The little houses on the prairie sleep eight and have fireplaces (kinda like a nice time-share in Vail), but the natives themselves snooze inside in warm beds (whaddya, nuts?). The Blackfeet cook up berry soup, wild game, and fry bread for guests, as well as any trout snagged while fly-fishing. The tribe also shows visitors the site of their sun dance ceremony and the cliffs where they drove buffalo off some 6,000 years ago. The Pueblos of northern New Mexico perform ceremonial dances for tourists as an alternative income generator to casinos, and the Navajos on the Arizona/Utah border (who've also said no dice to gambling) take visitors on horseback tours through the sandstone rocks of Monument Valley. The Hualapai of Arizona charge tourists to enter Grand Canyon West which happily sits on their reservation and the Utes of southwest Colorado take visitors on a tour of the Mesa Verde ruins. Finally, the Apaches of White Mountain, Arizona lead hunting trips and fishing excursions, perform their Sunrise Crown Dance, and demonstrate horseback riding and cavalry techniques. Watch "reality travel" sweep through tourism as more consumers realize it's a small world after all.

Bring a dose of reality to your category by offering consumers genuine experiences.

VACATIONS :
Fantasy Camps

"This will be a chance to laugh, to live some real excitement, to build new friendships, and to create memories that will last forever. Let us help you turn those dreams into reality."—SankeyRodeo.com

Got fantasy? Immediately after Chicago Cubs pitcher Randy Hundley conceived of a baseball camp for professional wannabees in the '80s, the fantasy genie was out of the bottle. Today there are a plethora of fantasy camp experiences to be had, most of them in the two occupations we consider our version of royalty, sports and entertainment. Although most major league baseball teams sponsor a fantasy camp—including a couple in Cuba and Japan—the cream of the crop is Cal Ripken's Grapefruit League (RipkenBaseball.com). For three days and about 8 Gs, it's as real as spring training gets in the bigs for batty men and women. Besides the instruction from current MLB players and managers, campers get their names on their uniforms and lockers and snack on David's Sunflower Seeds and Big League Chew shredded bubble gum, just like the pros do when they're not spitting tobacco juice on themselves. Michael Jordan's Senior Flight School at Caesar's Palace in Vegas, baby, is where 35+ers with serious hoop dreams and $15,000 can go downtown —make that try to go downtown—against His Airness.

There's also the Ultimate Golf Adventure for those wanting a PGA pro to correct that nasty slice or hook, and Spend A Day With Chris, where five large ones buys you some quality time with the Ice Queen herself at the Evert Tennis Academy in Boca. The Winter Olympics Challenge in Lake Placid offers the thrill of victory and agony of defeat (and maybe de feet) for those wishing to hurtle down a mountain in a luge or bobsled, and the Pro Wrestling Fantasy Camp in Philly is three days of smack-down mania. The Bull Riding Fantasy Camp in Rose Hill, Kansas puts boots, spurs, and chaps on city slickers wondering what it feels like to sit on an unusually angry piece of livestock for a few seconds. In music, there's the Triton Jazz Fantasy Camp, the Rock 'n Roll Fantasy Camp in, where else, Cleveland, and the Superstar Fantasy Camp where for $10,000 musicians get to record, produce, and edit their own CD in a Nashville studio. Look for us to slip on all shades of suede shoes to see what it's like to be king for a few days.

Contribute to consumers' experiential portfolio by offering fantasies related to your business.

TREND COMMANDMENT 4
Deliver Experience.

KA-CHING!

AUTOS
Market your vehicles not as a collection of disparate features but as a singular, unique experience.

BEAUTY
Recast your brand from a beauty product to a beauty experience.

ENTERTAINMENT & MEDIA
Flaunt your products' deliverables as multimedia experiences.

FASHION
Move beyond what clothes look like to what they make the wearer feel.

FINANCE
Create products and services wholly dedicated to the concept of experiential wealth.

FOOD & BEVERAGE

Add flavor to your brands by elevating taste to sensory experience.

HEALTHCARE

Position your brand's ability to heal as a life-affirming experience.

RETAIL

Buy and sell your inventory not as merchandise but as vessels of experience.

TECHNOLOGY

Defy time and space by bringing experiences to consumers when they can't make it to the experience.

TRAVEL & HOSPITALITY

Remember that the destination is incidental to the experience.

TREND COMMANDMENT 5

Get Smart.

TREND COMMANDMENT 5
Get Smart.

Thirsty for knowledge? Many of us are downright parched, eager to wet our cognitive whistles with any and kinds of learning, wisdom, and expertise. It being the Information Age, it's not surprising that information and, more specifically, smartness has emerged as one of the principal strands in our cultural DNA. Cogitate the idea that we are each trying to raise our cultural quotient or C.Q.—an individually defined concept of intelligence that determines our identity. Whether broad or narrow, our C.Q. is, above all, unique, laughing in the general direction of any standardized and easily measured form of intelligence like I.Q.. Smartness has infiltrated and infused everyday life, paralleling the evolution of the computer chip and the Internet. Just as technology has become The Big Story of our time and place, in other words, so has our quest to inscribe our own selves with different forms of intelligence. Technology has not only exponentially raised our ability to learn new things and share information but has provided an ideal cultural climate for smartness to germinate and pollinate. The impact of baby boomers too cannot be underestimated, as the most educated generation in history approaches learning as a lifelong process and passes on their values and aspirations to their kids.

The implication for marketers is pretty obvious: smarter is better. Smartness will only increase in worth and status in the future as our Information Age takes us to places difficult to imagine. Even more so than in the past, intelligence will separate the winners from the losers in our Darwinian economy, making it incumbent upon marketers to bestow smartness to consumers through products and services. Consider even deconstructing your brands' reasons-for-being into the kind and level of smartness it offers consumers. Such heady thinking may very well get you to the head of the class and leave your competitors wearing dunce caps in the corner. Here are some trends which illustrate how our collective cultural quotient is rising, hopefully sparking some ideas on how you can earn a gold star or get to stick your report card on your company's refrigerator.

THEORY:
Multiple Intelligence

"Who you are is more important than what you know."
—Philosophy of The New City School in St. Louis

It's been almost a decade since Harvard University professor Howard Gardner proposed his theory of multiple intelligences in his landmark book *Frames of Mind*. Educators around the world continue to put the theory into practice to formalize what good teachers knew intuitively—different students learn in different ways. Buoyed by our big cultural hug of diversity, i.e., that difference is good, and by brain research discussed in Daniel Goleman's 1995 bestseller, *Emotional Intelligence*, educators are increasingly recognizing that all kids are not cut from the same piece of brain matter. More teachers are creating optimum learning environments for success based on Gardner's multi-dimensional intelligence profiles, using different types of curricula and approaches to get Jacks and Jills up their own hills. The New City School, a pre-school to 6th grade independent institution in St. Louis, for example, is a leading advocate of multiple intelligence (MI), knowing that kids (and adults, for that matter) best acquire knowledge and process information when using the type of intelligence they are most comfortable with versus one imposed on them. MI not only allows children to discover their strengths and abilities but can help little learners solve problems and work with others. As a refresher (don't worry, there won't be a pop quiz), Gardner's eight types of intelligence are: (1) linguistic (a sensitivity to the meaning and order of words); (2) logical/mathematical (a reliance on reason, patterns, order, and numbers); (3) visual/spatial (a keen perception of the physical world); (4) bodily/kinesthetic (skill in moving one's body and/or objects); (5) musical (a strong sense of pitch, melody, rhythm, and tone), (6) interpersonal (a considerable understanding of people and relationships); (7) intrapersonal (easy access to one's own emotions); and (8) naturalist (an ability to observe, classify, and compare information, specifically plants and animals). The concept of MI has been picked up by marketers like Vivendi Universal Publishing which, through its Knowledge Adventure® brand, targets JumpStart™ educational software to teachers and parents wishing to match content with a child's respective learning style. At JumpStart.com, visitors can determine a student's preferred style of learning, and at Education.com, they can find out which kinds of intelligence famous folks used to succeed in their particular field. Look out as a generation raised on diversity in thinking grows up and wields their multiple intelligences.

Think different by using multiple forms of intelligence in your marketing communications.

EDUCATION:
Specialty Camps

"Empowering People to Choose Wealth, Prosperity and Abundance!"—Mission of The Money Camp in Santa Barbara

For many kids, smartness has oozed from the school year into the summer, confirming that one can never be too young to begin developing an area of expertise. Some 10 million kids head off to nearly 12,000 summer camps every year in this country, an increasing number of them to specialty camps. While learning how to make a lanyard and dribble a basketball was enough for a previous generation of happy campers, kids today are gaining skills in computers (and hacking), filmmaking, astronaut training, rocket building, spying, and modeling. Three dozen or so 11 to 18 year olds head out to Shelter Island, Long Island every summer to practice, practice, practice at the Perlman Music Program led by virtuoso fiddler Itzhak Perlman. At Sports Broadcasting Mini-camp, kids meet professional broadcasters, tour TV studios, make demo tapes, and, presumably, learn how to buy exceptionally bad sports jackets and how to blow dry their hair on the "poofy" setting. Even spa camp is available for kids interested in the fine art of how to enjoy a facial, manicure, or pedicure. But it is business camps, and especially entrepreneur camps, that perhaps are the clearest indicators of our current impetus to instill savviness and success among Generations Y and Z. At Camp Venture Creek, a non-profit organization in Nevada City, California, for example, kids from 8 to 14 learn how to become successful entrepreneurs from those who did it themselves. Retired technology entrepreneur Dan Lynch along with top execs from companies like Sun Microsystems teach kids—mostly from low-income families there on scholarships—how to make money doing what they love to do. During the daily 90 minute program called KidBiz, wee wheeler dealers raise their entrepreneurial quotient by leaning how to set goals and take risks. And at Camp $tart-Up at the Dana Hall School in Wellesley, Massachusetts, teenage girls learn how to write business plans from successful women entrepreneurs. Its sister camp, Summer $tock, leads girls through the byzantine, male-dominated world of investing and finance. Especially for those not on the inside track, specialty camps are acorns of smartness that one day will turn many younger folks into big oaks in their chosen profession.

Pitch your tent in smart camp by offering products and services grounded in junior achievement.

ONLINE: E-Learning

Let your fingers do the smart walking. After getting grazed in the dot-com drive-by, e-learning is thriving as more of us log on to get smarter. E-learning will be a $12–$14 billion market by 2004, according to Booz Allen Hamilton, with much of that to come from corporate training programs. Rather than fly executives around to traditional classroom settings, IBM and other companies are saving big bucks by putting most of its training courses online, and more certification and compliance requirements are being met over the Net. E-learners take a test online and, assuming they pass, click on "Print" to receive their certificate instantly. The federal government is, somewhat surprisingly, on the e-learning fast track, one of President (and Harvard MBA) Bush's 24 "e-government" initiatives outlined in his Management Agenda. The US Office of Personnel Management's e-learning website (Opm.gov) offers feds one-stop access to training products and services, helping agencies build a brainier workforce. The 30,000 employees of the US Embassy staff too are ambassadors of e-learning, taking some 500 self-paced, Web-based tutorials in information technology. With its SmartForce live monitor capability, the Department of State's Foreign Service Institute allows e-learners in 250 different sites around the world to ask questions on the fly via e-mail or instant messaging. Sharper universities are also attending e-state by targeting more online education programs to undergraduates, grad students, and professionals. eCornell, the online distance learning unit of Cornell University, offers a certificate from its prestigious School of Hotel Administration, and some 50 cops and secret agents from Alaska to Virginia are getting a Master's degree in Criminal Justice from Boston University's online division. UMassOnline saw enrollment rise 58% and revenues increase 82% in 2002 with its 30 graduate and undergraduate programs, which include more than 275 continuing ed courses from UMass at Amherst and Lowell, Boston University, and Dartmouth College. Students love having an electronic option, allowing them to study on their own schedules, keep their full-time jobs, and increase their course load by saving time getting to and from class. With the help of chat rooms and voice and data conferencing software, there's a surprising amount of interaction with classmates and professors, e-students report, as many are likely to say things online one might not when F-2-F (as we all know all too well). Expect more corporate training, university level, and adult education courses to go online as organizations of all stripes embrace an "anytime, anywhere" philosophy of learning.

Go to school on e-learning by delivering smartness to consumers via your website.

FAMILY :
Family History

"Your family story is waiting."—***Genealogy.com slogan***

What's your story? If you're one of the 80 million or so Americans actively seeking information about their ancestors, your story is unfolding. We're on a family history treasure hunt rivaled only by that of the late 19th century when high society WASPS frantically proved (or invented) their pedigrees to distance themselves from the immigrant riff-raff. This movement, however, which can be traced back to the "Roots" phenomenon of the mid-70s, is as populist as it gets, spread across all social classes wanting to know everything there is to know about their family's story. The Internet has, of course, opened up the floodgates to the past, offering boatloads on information about the other branches and leaves on the family tree. At sites such as MyFamily.com, Genealogy.com (part of A&E Television Networks), AncestryPlus.com, and FamilySearch.org (run by genealogical gurus Church of Jesus Christ of the Latter-day Saints), e-sleuths piece together the fragments of their family history puzzle. And at EllisIsland.org, visitors scour through some 500 million pieces of digital information to learn more about relatives who were part of the huddled masses yearning to breathe free. So many users logged onto EllisIsland.org when it was first launched that Lycos's server was knocked on its digital ass, and now some

150,000 visitors a week land on the site's shores. Not only can you create a digital Family History Scrapbook using tools the site provides, but one can view or buy copies of original passenger manifests and photos of the ship great-grandpa arrived on. After researching family letters, diaries, and bibles and using online resources to create the trunk and a few limbs of a family tree, some add branches by making a pilgrimage to ancestors' homeland. Interviewing relatives who can tell their side of the story is essential for the serious family historian, often requiring one to make a journey back across the big pond to hear from the descendants of those who missed the boat. Walking in the same steps or sitting in the same church pew that one's great-great-great-greats did centuries ago is an immensely powerful experience that helps people see their own life as just one link of a very long chain. Hard-cores then write social histories of their family, often self-publishing and distributing them to the rest of the clan for posterity. Family history is a passionate form of knowledge that reflects our deep yearning to establish meaningful links with the past in order to connect our identity dots. Expect even more of us to get smarter by learning the backstory on who we are.

Root yourself in making consumers smarter and watch your ship come in.

HOBBIES:
Amateur Astronomy

Searching for cosmic knowledge? More people are, and are finding it just by looking up. As *The New York Times* reported, amateur astronomy is reaching new heights of popularity as celestial bodies boldly explore space, the final frontier. It is remarkable that it has taken this long for astronomy to take off given that it represents perhaps the ultimate form of intelligence, revolving around nothing less than the workings of the universe. But until recently, professional astronomers had dibs on high-quality telescopes, forcing amateurs to build their own. With professional quality telescopes now more affordable, however, lots more neophytes are seeing stars, especially families looking for an activity offering an infinite constellation of knowledge. Comet-fever too has stirred interest in amateur astronomy, most recently when Hale-Bopp bopped its way across the Milky Way in 1997. And with the world's largest virtual reality simulator, the New Hayden Planetarium at the American Museum of Natural History's Rose Center for Earth and Space is also creating new moonies. Three million people listened to Tom Hanks narrate the Center's inaugural Space Show, "Passport to the Universe," in the two years it played, and now star trekkers are flocking to hear Harrison Ford present "The Search for Life: Are We Alone?". At the planetarium's Big Bang sphere, Maya Angelou takes visitors to the beginning of time for a multi-sensory re-creation of the first moments of the universe. In such a heavenly climate, it's not surprising that both kids and adults are throwing star or sky parties, the most stellar being those that are in Nowheresville, as far from city lights as possible. Pick up a mobile or backyard observatory from HomeDome.com and you're in for a show that is light years greater than the greatest show on Earth. Astronomy.com is the place to scope out gear, get tips on how to catch a rising star with a camera, and check out the picture of the day from tonight's sky (maybe it's Uranus!). Astronomy puts the black holes of this mortal plane into perspective, reminding us that all that has happened, is happening, and will happen here on Earth is smaller than the tiniest freckle on the pinky toenail of the universe.

Be a star in your galaxy by satisfying our innate curiosity about where no man has gone before.

TRAVEL:
Learning Vacations

"Unless vacation travel is a learning experience, unless it leaves you a bit different from what you were when you began, it is, in my view, a pointless physical exercise."
—Arthur Frommer, travel guru

Noticed that no one takes the kinds of vacations Americans used to take? When was the last time you or someone you know, say, laid on a beach drinking pina coladas out of pineapple husks for a couple of weeks? In the Information Age, even vacations are viewed as opportunities to learn or try something new, to use one's brain rather than soak it in Bacardi 151. Folks who want to learn the ins and outs of innkeeping, for example, are heading to the Elizabeth Point Lodge in Florida's Amelia Island for three days of "B&B Bootcamp," while the Frank Lloyd Wright Preservation Trust in Oak Park, Illinois lets prairie schoolers break new ground by learning how to plan and design one's dream house. Seaworld's "Trainer-for-a-day" program instructs guests in the care and feeding of marine mammals, and L.L. Bean's Outdoor Discover Schools teaches folks in flannel how to photograph wildlife aboard a windjammer in Penobscot Bay. Opportunities to get smarter by learning more about a different corner of the world also abound, a clear sign that Americans are pursuing knowledge wherever and whenever they can get it. Hordes of gringos are headed to tiny villages in Guatemala, for example, to learn Spanish native-style. Visitors get one-on-one lessons at Eco-Escuela de Espanol, and then practice in town where it's Spanish-only. Not only is it cheaper than Berlitz, but travelers come away with a life experience they will never forget. Interhostel, an organization sponsored by the University of New Hampshire, has been offering learning vacations to older peripatetics for over twenty years. For about 3Gs, 50+ers get a two-week immersive experience in the history and culture of any one of a hundred or so different places. University faculty are typically along for the ride, providing context for what travelers see and do. One of the more popular trips is to the Dios de los Muertos ritual in Mexico, where locals take the remains of their dearly departed relatives home for a few hours of R&R. Travelers get to join in the fun, getting a first-hand look at an entirely different cultural perspective of death. Interaction with locals is one of the primary themes of learning vacations, a controversial practice but one that undoubtedly adds a deeper layer to any traveling experience. Dedicated to delivering real knowledge about the real world in real time, learning vacations offer the best souvenir of all—personal growth.

Jump on consumers' mission of "wanderlust with a purpose."

RECREATION:
Chess Clubs

Ready for the multitasking, minivan driving Chess Mom? Chess is chasing down soccer as an activity for kids as one of the world's most ancient games finds new fans, more of whom came on board after seeing it come to life in *Harry Potter and the Sorcerer's Stone*. Chess programs are increasingly holding court in elementary schools, high schools, and colleges, with some kids even getting up when the rooster crows to get in a match before their morning classes. The U.S. Chess Federation reports that its scholastic membership multiplied eight times since 1990 as more of these brain trusts were formed in schools across the country. New York City's Chess-in-the-Schools program is the largest of its kind, with some 38,000 kindergartners to 8th graders in 160 schools regularly moving pieces around a little square board. And forget the idea that chess is just for the elite. Many poor kids and minorities are 21st century knights, queens, and kings, often sending kids wearing blue blazers and rep ties packing back to Hogwarts and other private academies. The club from Morningside Elementary in Brownsville, Texas, for example, placed second at the junior varsity level in the last national tournament, proving that income, race, and

ethnicity are pawns in this game of strategic, analytical wits. Boys from the hood at Miami's Jackson High, wearing shorts phatter than anything from the House of Large Sizes, are building a chess dynasty, adding to its trophy case full of national titles nearly every year. Playing chess is also proving to raise academic performance, as each move is an exercise in critical thinking, decision-making, and problem-solving. As a metaphor for life, where every action has consequences, chess helps instill self-confidence and an ethic of success, training kids to think ahead, plan for the future, and consider one's options before making one's move. Almost 20 American universities are now offering full scholarships to recruit chess mates as a means to boost their academic reputation and public image and to compete with the Ivy League for the best and brightest students. Watch chess catch up to major sports programs as more parents and educators prioritize brains over brawn.

Be a knight in shining armor by enabling consumers to get smarter in the game of life.

TRANSPORTATION:
Smart Cars

The major problem with cars and trucks: They tend to hit other cars and trucks. 10 million people are hurt in traffic accidents every year, in fact, according to the National Highway Traffic Safety Administration, and hospital bills and property damage from accidents account for 3% of the world's gross domestic product ($200 billion in the U.S. alone) annually, according to the Organization for Economic Cooperation and Development. This demolition derby could perhaps have been predicted given that when there exactly two cars in Kansas (82,282 square miles) in the beginning of the 20th century they somehow found a way to crash into each other. One hundred years later, engineers are finally figuring out that they're going to have to make vehicles a lot smarter than their drivers. Smart cars that stop before they hit another vehicle, grandma, or Fluffy or pre-deploy airbags if a crash is unavoidable have the metal on the pedal as ultra-wideband sensors come on board over the next five or so years. Radar or lidar (light detecting and ranging) systems on the bumpers are already optional equipment on Mercedes, Lexus, and Infiniti, warning drivers of impending disaster with beeps or dashboard lights. Interestingly, trucks are further ahead on the smart curve than cars, with more than 10,000 semis now rollin', rollin', rollin' with radar-based collision-warning systems on board. These "adaptive cruise control" systems reduce accidents by 70% by alerting good buddies and inducing the brakes to kick into gear. Engineers are now testing the idea of multi-vehicle platoons—yep, convoys—where trucks automatically cruise along just like train cars. And at its Human Interface Lab in Tempe, Arizona, Motorola is hot on the dusty trail of the next generation of vehicles that will leave today's in the rear-view mirror. With its souped-up 4-door Saturn, motorheads are taking up to 130 performance measurements, creating a host of worst case scenarios and then figuring out how best to relay the bad news (e.g., you're about to hit that really big tree or Bambi) to the driver. Sensors will remind those using the road as a slalom course to stay on the straight and narrow and tell tailgaters to get off that next car's butt. Audio e-mail via cell phone or PDA will allow drivers to keep their hands on the wheel, as will voice-recognition stereo systems. Smart cars are the next logical evolution of what is arguably the most influential (for better and worse) artifact of the last century. Sit back and enjoy the ride as seeing the U.S.A. in your Chevrolet gets a lot smarter and safer.

Put yourself in the driver's seat with smart technologies that save consumers' lives and money.

FASHION:
Smart Clothing

After a few millennia of basically laying on your body like a lox, clothing is on the hem of revolutionary change. Various technologies are converging to make clothing much more than something to keep you warm and to signify your social class. Clothing which "thinks," i.e., changes functionality based on conditions or performs different tasks, is gradually making its way to the marketplace and your bod. A little more than 25 years after Gore-Tex, the first waterproof fabric that could breathe, made its wicky debut, a new generation of materials is making cotton and wool look downright sheepish. Gateway Technology's Outlast thermal insulation, for example, adjusts to one's skin temperature, while DuPont is developing garments that can expand and contract as well as change temperature and color. Motorola and Burlington Industries are exploring high-tech fabrics that can neutralize body odor, monitor vital signs, and even locate wearers by satellite (begging the question, "Is that a GPS in your pocket or are you just glad to see me?"). Sensatex is also working on a shirt that can keep track of athletes' heart and respiration rates and body temperatures, while Hanes has launched an early salvo into what will inevitably be a monster business, the integration of health, beauty, and fashion (HBF?). The fabric in Hanes's new Body Enhancers "cosmetic hosiery" is embedded with tea and microencapsulated grapefruit seed extract that treats the appearance of cellulite, just the beginning of a coming flood of clothes with healing properties. Levi's and Lee's are also thinking small with subatomic nanotechnology, each offering Nano-Tex khakis that aggressively resist stains and shrinking. Such innovations are bikini pants, however, compared to the muumuu merger of fashion and information technology. "Wearware"—technology-enabled apparel—is on the digital loom, with companies like Phillips Design investing in R&D for wearable electronics. Using polymers with super-thin films of silicon, textile researchers in Scotland are developing clothing which generates its own source of electricity to power cell phones or MP3 players without batteries. As well, the Brussels-based research group Starlab is partnering with Adidas, Levi Strauss, and Samsonite (as well as NASA) to integrate computing capabilities into fabrics and fibers and, after introducing a ski parka with a GSM (global walkie-talkie) feature, Reima plans to offer apparel with a built-in web browser. Wear intelligence on your sleeve as different forms of smart clothing make their way to our cultural closet.

Weave intelligence into your business through products with "thinking" capabilities.

HOME:
Smart Appliances

That dumb-as-a-box-of-cold-cuts refrigerator and its electric cousins are about to get a lot smarter. Home appliances are on the cusp of making a quantum leap forward as manufacturers hook them up to the Internet and turn them into, essentially, machines that can think. The first generation of information appliances (IAs) blew a major fuse, but consumers are slowly coming around the idea (12.4 million households are willing to adopt a home network, according to the Yankee Group) and marketers have gone to school on their mistakes. Westinghouse, for example, is rolling out a line of networked home appliances powered by Microsoft Windows CE.NET which promise to take some of the work out of housework. Turn on that coffee maker, oven, or bread maker with a click of your mouse and dinner will be on the table before you can say, "Rosie Jetson." Whirlpool too is stirring up the technology pot with its i-enabled "Gold" brand that's going right into new construction, as is Zenith and Samsung with their lines. Smart appliances are already selling like kim-chee in Korea, often an early indicator of what will ultimately be popular in the States. Air conditioning manufacturers like Lennox and Carrier are testing systems that can be activated via the Web, bringing cold comfort to homeowners the second they open the door. Other innovations coming to your kitchen soon are refrigerators which keep track of expiration dates on foods, microwaves which decide how long they should cook items, and even garbage cans which read "data" and generate a new shopping list. Equally if not more important to the convenience factor are the energy savings that this new generation of home appliances may offer one day. Washers and dryers, such as those in development by Kenmore and Maytag, will have the smarts to conserve water and determine how hot it should be, while dishwashers will decide for themselves when to start the run cycle based on electricity usage in the community. Also exciting are the remote possibilities for service, meaning the days when one has to wait for that heavyset guy with the unfortunately low riding pants to show (or not show) up may soon be over. Expect the wealthy and the gotta-have-it-firsts to be on the front end of the smart appliance bell curve as it starts to ring.

Heat up your business by building in intelligence to your products and services.

TREND COMMANDMENT 5
Get Smart.

KA-CHING!

AUTOS
Spend as much time thinking about your vehicles' brains as their bodies to make safety first.

BEAUTY
Define beauty as an innate human intelligence that your brands can help bring out.

ENTERTAINMENT & MEDIA
Position your products and services as a form of cultural intelligence in today's entertainment-driven society.

FASHION
Develop clothes that can change functionality based on different conditions.

FINANCE
Show how choosing one of your advisors is one of the smartest decisions investors can make.

FOOD & BEVERAGE

Elevate your brand's reason-for-being from tasty morsel to brain agent.

HEALTHCARE

Express wellness as a state of intelligence in which mind, body, and spirit commune.

RETAIL

Create environments that allow shoppers to get a little smarter each time they visit.

TECHNOLOGY

Exploit the incredible power of technology to inform, educate, and make learning fun.

TRAVEL & HOSPITALITY

Present traveling as learning experiences about the world and oneself.

TREND COMMANDMENT 6

Nurture Nature.

TREND COMMANDMENT 6
Nurture Nature.

It was sometime in the 1990s when I fully realized that our flirtatious, on-again-off-again relationship with Mother Nature had become a hot and heavy romance. The W Hotel in New York was putting boxes of different varieties of grass in rooms along with watering cans so that guests could take care of their personal plot of land during their stay. The SoHo Grand hotel had long (and continues to) put goldfish in guest's rooms, but this was something new and intriguing, at least for someone with nothing better to think about. Were plants now the children of the '90s, perhaps even displacing pets? Was Flora gaining the upper limb on Fauna? Well no, but something certainly was a'budding, given other green goings-on. Supermarkets were starting to stock up on organic foods, the National Parks were making Club Med seem dowdy, and the Green Party was becoming something more than a radical acorn. It was clear that the seeds of the ecology movement of the 1970s had begun to bloom as a new, more mature wave of environmentalism swept across America like tumbleweed. We are now living in truly verdant times as all generations embrace nature as a secular form of spiritualism. Our postwar love of and trust in chemistry and weird science is as dead as the Cold War, replaced by a desire to breathe, eat, and wear nature as much as possible and dwell in its greeny goodness. We want, in short, to go back to the garden.

So what does this bed of roses mean to you? Because today's environmentalism movement is different than previous ones—part of the system rather than in opposition to the system—marketers have an unparalleled opportunity to escort consumers directly to Eden. We want to celebrate nature both at home and away from home, meaning that green marketing can be a kudzu-like business strategy. Think of these trends as natural fertilizer to sprinkle onto your brands, plans, and programs to watch your garden grow.

GARDENING:
Organic Gardening

"Man is a part of nature, and his war against nature is inevitably a war against himself." —Rachel Carson

If you can't beat nature, more gardeners are saying, better join it. After centuries of trying to conquer the land, more recently with chemical fertilizers and pesticides, we're now increasingly choosing to become allies with it through organic gardening. Organic gardeners shun modern agriculture's chemistry set, believing that nuking plants and the soil not only leaves toxic residues on the food we eat but damages the eco-system as a whole. Not that long ago the exclusive realm of people whose favorite band was Peter, Paul, and Mary, organic gardening today is the approach of choice for masters of their backyard domains. Organic foods ring in about $10 billion a year at retail, no longer relegated to that health food store near the university run by a chick named Moonbeam. The phenomenal growth of organics—900% in the U.S. since 1990—has spawned a dedicated organic movement or lifestyle whose loudest voice is *Organic Style*, a magazine which has already scooped up a half million subscribers. Organic gardeners work in harmony with nature, viewing their piece of land and everything in it as somehow interdependent. They add only natural matter to the soil, using locally available resources like grass clippings, fall leaves, or kitchen scraps whenever possible, and choose plants that are appropriate to the site's climate and conditions. They believe that poisons used to kill garden pests also harm the good-guy bugs and birds and that our obsession with getting rid of weeds is misdirected and ultimately futile. So rather than use synthetics to add nutrients to the soil, control insects, stop disease, and kill weeds, purists employ biodegradable "biocides" like garlic and roots, use manure as fertilizer, and bring in natural pest fighters like ladybugs, preying mantises, and companion plants. The result is healthier plants, which taste better, store longer, and cope with insects, weather, and disease without harming people or the environment. People who try an organically grown fruit or vegetable typically react as if eating the food for the first time, a sensory wake-up call that commercial growers' priorities are shelf life and appearance versus taste and health. With the USDA finally implementing national standards to end the confusion and varying opinions about the requirements, definitions, and labeling of organic foods, get ready for more of us to get in the garden bed with Mother Nature.

Flunk chemistry class in your category and, unlike in high school, enjoy it this time around.

RETAIL:
Farmer's Markets

Want to make those trucked in fruits and vegetables at your local supermarket turn green with envy? Make a beeline to one of the 2,800 farmer's markets scattered across the country. The number of farmer's markets is rising a healthy 10% each year, according to the USDA, as more consumers from coast-to-coast get down to earth with right-off-the-vine produce. These al fresco trips to bountiful offer direct contact with the growers, taking out a few links in the food chain which means not only better tasting but more nutritious food. For a breath of fresh air in New York, swing by the Union Square Greenmarket in Greenwich Village on a Saturday and you're likely to find some Rome and motsu apples, Yukon gold potatoes, and portobello mushrooms that will stir the soul of even the most jaded taste buds. Dig the quinces, rutabagas, and burdock root, ingredients that are snarfed up by the city's best chefs and turned into culinary masterpieces. One simply must belly up to the market's "sprout bar," a cornucopia of over a dozen varieties of sprouts which would impress even the Jolly Green Giant's diminutive friend. Left coasters too are bypassing the Piggly Wiggly for the real thing at the Santa Monica farmer's market. Open Saturday mornings and located at Arizona Avenue between 2nd and 4th Streets, this orgasmic vegopolis serves up the freshest grub this side of Eden. Check out a variety of wild mushrooms "hand-picked from the forest" like matsutake, chanterelles, and my personal favorite, chicken of the woods. Lettuce too there is an exercise in salivary heaven, with upland cress, red chard, Osaka mustard, and tat-soi eager to become your next salad (at $7 a precious pound). Serve up some dried Fuji apples, honeyloupes, supersweet kabocha squash, or red rose creaming potatoes at your next do and you are sure to be named king or queen for the day. Lowly sprouts are miracles of nature here too, with buckwheat, fanugreek, and kamut seedlings able to turn that first course into a celebration of chlorophyll. In addition to the heavy Asian influence (mizuna, komatsuma ake, or diakon radishes the size of trombones), organics are the order of the day, with chemical-free onions, squash, eggplant, jujube, melons, pumpkins, and pomegranates ready to steal your healthy heart away. No less than 75% of the produce at the Santa Fe farmer's market is organically grown, bringing some old world flavor back to some 5,000 new agers every Saturday. Expect more of us to go back to the garden via the sensory heavens that are farmer's markets.

Root out opportunity with products that push the green envelope.

FOOD & BEVERAGE:
Raw Food

What's on the front burner in cooking? Not cooking. A raw (also "living") foods movement is sprouting as more adventurous foodies sit down at nature's table. With pretty much every ethnic food now colonized, bam!—along comes something truly revolutionary. A sub-culture of health food or next generation of vegetarians, raw foodists pass on anything that's heated at more than 120 degrees Fahrenheit (that would be "warm" to we non-scientists). Eat-it-raws believe that cooking kills off nutrients and enzymes, and that food in the buff provides the body with more energy and stamina. Because it is easier to digest, adherents say, raw food extends one's youth and deters disease. Although many scientists have a T-bone to pick with such claims, raw foods are gradually being embraced by big name chefs and those who appreciate more adventurous cuisine. There are about 20 restaurants in the U.S. intentionally undercooking food, with Chicago's Charlie Trotter and the Bay Area's Roxanne Klein the best well known cooks whipping up gourmet food that's never seen the inside of an oven. And when prepared by a chef who knows his/her way around a kitchen, raw foods are hardly limited to a platter of crudite or dinner salad. With some creativity, pizza, pasta, enchiladas, and even burgers can be prepared with no baking, boiling, broiling, or frying, as can more tasty delicacies. Try, for example, the $100 five-course dinner at Roobios Tea House in Los Angeles that includes dishes like macadamia ravioli and your tongue will be wagging for more raw. There's over a month wait to get into one of Roxanne's 64 seats at her eponymous restaurant in Larkspur, where dishes like pad thai and ratatouille await in raw splendor. Celebrities such as Alicia Silverstone and Demi Moore are nibbling on raw foods, as are another estimated 1 million Americans. The German airline Lufthansa now offers a raw food meal upon request for travelers wanting a healthier alternative to wienerschnitzel or knockwurst at 36,000 feet. And now very comfortable eating sushi and sashimi, Americans are even getting comfortable with the idea of eating raw eggs, a dietary taboo since the salmonella scare of the mid-1990s.

Restaurants like Craftbar in New York and the Water Grill in L.A. are taking the raw egg plunge, adding the slimy ingredient to bruschetta and angel hair pasta. Look for raw foods to pop up more often on America's table as we try to snarf down nature in its purest form.

OPPORTUNITY

Undercook your products to feature nature on your marketing menu.

CAUSE: Eco-Activism

"It is companies, not advocacy groups, that will create the technologies needed to save the environment."
—Jonathan Woolf, ex-Greenpeacer

And what were you doing on April 22, 1970? You'd remember if you were one of the 20 million Americans who demonstrated for a healthier planet on the first Earth Day, the birth of the modern environmental movement. Today, eco-activism is lusher than ever, with another generation of greenies committed to sustainable biodiversity, conservation of native plants and wildlife, and combating nuclear energy, polluters, and global warming. Donations to U.S. environmental groups hit $6.4 billion this past year and are up 50% in the past five years, according to the American Association of Fundraising Council Trust for Philanthropy, which is a big part of the reason air and water are cleaner now than in decades. Better known organizations such as the National Audubon Society and the Sierra Club and lesser known ones like the Environmental Defense Fund, Earth Force, EcoFuture, River Watch, Eden Foundation, and Animal Alliance are all dedicated in their own way to making the world a greener place. Time's Up! is helping make New York a less toxic city through events like its

Central Park Traffic Calming Ride, when bicyclists make their presence known by taking over a car lane. You ain't seen nothin' until you've seen a New York cabbie huffing and puffing behind a hundred Huffies. The giant redwood of all eco-activism, however, is the international "direct-action" organization Greenpeace. The 1990s were a bad decade for Greenpeace, with membership falling from 1 million to 300,000 and the entire board of directors resigning because of internal feuding. But thanks to President Bush the sequel, Greenpeace is back with a vengeance, attacking global warming with full vigor and lots of cash. George W.'s less-than-environmentally-friendly energy plan and rejection of a treaty to combat global warming gave the organization renewed purpose and a sense of urgency to promote sustainable energy and end the world's reliance on fossil fuels. Greenpeacers are once again doing what they do best, like dumping five tons of coal in front of Vice President Cheney's house. (They cleaned it up.) The organization is also working with scientists, mediators, and lawyers, using, well, more tidy tactics to get multi-national corporations to give a hoot and not pollute. Watch eco-activism bloom as Generations Y and Z pick up the green ball and run with it.

Make your brands greener to make your balance sheet greener.

AGRICULTURE: Hemp Movement

What are many eco-activists wearing (and maybe smoking)? Hemp—the natural fiber that serves as a central rallying point for the noble cause of renewable and sustainable agriculture. Since 1937, the heyday of *Reefer Madness*, industrial hemp has been illegal to grow in America, classified as a drug under the Controlled Substance Act because of the plant's ne'er-do-well cousin, marijuana, even though you'd have to smoke a silo of the stuff to catch a buzz. But hemp was once a staple of American agriculture, used since the 1600s for ropes, sails, riggings, fabrics, and oil. George Washington grew hemp, Betsy Ross used it to sew her flags, and Benjamin Franklin owned a hemp mill. Although revived in World War II when millions of "Hemp for Victory" acres were grown for military use, the war against what's been called "nature's perfect plant" was again declared by Uncle Sam. Many farmers and marketers are now stoked, however, to persuade lawmakers to deregulate hemp because of its value as a versatile, "environmentally benign" natural resource and raw material. 25,000 products can be made with hemp, according to the North American Industrial Hemp Council, from cosmetics to auto parts. And just because hemp is illegal to grow in the States, it doesn't mean you can't wear it, cuddle it, eat it, drink it, or sell it at weed-friendly stores like Fred Segal or Urban Outfitters. Scores of companies from around the world market hemp-based clothing and other products, and American manufacturers are importing seeds 'n stems from Canada. Adidas, for example, makes hemp sneakers that are groovier than anything to come off Nike's assembly line, and Headcase offers a line of, what else, hemp hats. Hemp jewelry, clothing, crafts, and housewares can be had from companies like Dank Forest, a self-described "hemporium," and pretzels, beer, and energy bars made with hemp oil are purportedly hempalicious. Hemp shower curtains can be had from Real Goods, hemp-citronella candles from Way Out Wax, and hemp-flax paper from straighter-than-an-arrow Staple's. For kids, there's hemp diapers and wool soakers from What's Hempenin' Baby and a "cute and huggable" hemp teddy from Aware Bear. There's hemp chew and play toys for that hep cat or dog from a company named DogNip, and believe it or not, a motorcycle powered by hemp. As government officials eventually come to their senses about this benevolent outlaw, watch hemp to start really smokin'.

Plant some natural seeds in your products to grow a bountiful cash crop.

HOBBIES:
Bird Watching

Shh! Is that a hooded warbler? A gray-cheek thrush? Or perhaps just a blackbird singing in the dead of night? If you're one of the millions of bird watchers, you'd probably know. Bird watching and genealogy are running beak to beak to be America's second favorite hobby, each giving gardening a run for its pole position money. Whether sticking to their own backyards, traveling to migratory rest stops in the spring, or journeying to tropical jungles, bird watchers are cuckoo for ornithology. Why have the number of birders jumped 155% (faster than any other outdoor activity) over the last decade, according to National Public Radio? "Bagging" a bird, as tweetie-pies put it, is a way to reconnect with nature and, unlike 99.9% of entertainment today, offers surprises and unpredictability. Many birders view the hobby as an opportunity to build a lifetime collection of sightings or actually "hearings," as wiser owls can identify a particular species just by its call or song. Bye-bye birdees make a pilgrimage to regions of the country where migratory birds take five, putting a feather in their caps if they bag one they've never seen or heard before. The Great Texas Birding Classic is an avian Superbowl, awarding $50,000 to the team which spots the most species (the money is then donated to the winners' preferred bird sanctuary or protected habitat). Birds of a feather from around the world post Rare Bird Alerts (RBAs) on the Internet to notify others to look up (check out VirtualBird.com for a real hoot). Others are winging their way to tropical bird workshops in Latin and South America, in search of exotic parrots and toucans which stay put for the summer. One doesn't have to go far, however, to enjoy the company of our fine feathered friends. Sales of birdfeeders, birdhouses, and birdbaths are soaring as suburbanites check out the chicks, and urbanites have their eagle eyes set on city chirpers. The Nature Conservancy leads bird walks through New York's Central Park which offer a glimpse of an egret or pintail duck, and Gothamites regularly are scoping out an apartment building at Fifth Avenue and 74th Street where a family of red-tail hawks (led by ornicelebrity Pale Male) nest. Realizing they are in the catbird's seat, the National Audubon Society plans to open 1,000 nature centers in lower income communities by 2020 in order to create a younger, more diverse constituency for conservation. Keep a sharp lookout for bird watching as we rely on nature to keep us grounded.

Celebrate the wonders of nature to attract flocks of consumers.

PETS:
Holistic Pet Care

You and your pup check into a dog-friendly hotel like the W at Union Square in New York. Suddenly, Princess's allergies start acting up, and you realize you left all her herbal remedies at home. What do you do? Ring the Bow Wow Concierge, of course, on call 24 hours a day to treat dogs with THC (Tender Holistic Care). Pets can also get an organic meal, Shiatsu massage, a hot oil fur treatment at the W, clear enough proof that many of us want to treat our best friends just like ourselves when it comes to wellness. As integrated or complementary healthcare continues to gain acceptance among those with oppositional thumbs, holistic pet care too is on the rise, offering lots of dogs and cats a better quality of life. More pets are just saying no to drugs, their vets opting for alternative therapies which can be less costly, as effective, and safer than prescriptive medicine. Antihistamines and steroids are not the best choice for certain pets, making pet healthcare workers shift from a strict pharmaceutical approach to a broader one dedicated to different kinds of healing. Herbs especially are being used for four-legged sickies although, as for humans, type and dosage are critical, individually-defined factors. Aloe vera is now commonly prescribed to treat a canine boo-boo or feline ouchy, and catnip has long been used to calm down upper puppies and krazy kats as well as relieve their muscle spasms, diarrhea, and gas. Dandelion is a popular choice for allergies, arthritis, and constipation, while garlic is often prescribed for asthma, diabetes, or fleas. For cognitive disorder, the quadruped version of Alzheimer's, vets go with choline, lecithin, or gingko biloba. Acupuncture too is increasingly applied to dogs and cats, complementing a chemotherapy regimen for pets with leukemia or cancer. Hard evidence, along with about 2,000 years of history in China, suggests that poking needles into any body's radiant energy fields not just relieves pain but can boost immune systems and improve organ functions. Admittedly not a cure-all, poochie puncture is more likely to be elected when surgery is not an option for older or seriously ill dogs. Pointy permutations are aquapuncture, which injects medicinal herbs and/or vitamins into that aching dog or cat, and moxa-bustion, where warm Chinese herbs are rubbed onto the patient's coat. With the way a society treats its animal companions a key indicator of its relative health, keep a sharp eye on holistic pet care as a general check-up on American culture.

Give consumers a natural choice in your product category and watch the fur fly.

HOUSEWORK:
Natural Cleaners

Mmm...Is that jasmine lily fragrance you're wearing? Oops, sorry, it's just the dish soap. Natural cleaning products, many of them aromatherapeutic, are bubbling up, turning housework into a less toxic affair and even Zen-like experience. Cleaning products are finally waking up from their 1950s nap, when rubber gloved moms white tornadoed and pine soled dirt and germs back to the Stone Age. The idea that chemistry is next to godliness is changing, however, as more of us make our houses and everything in them spic 'n span with environmentally friendly products. Brands like OxiClean, Free and Natural Laundry Detergent, and SunFeather Natural Soap are dye–and perfume-free, while others like Heather's Natural Organic Cleaning Products and Citri-Solv leave irritating lye and ammonia out but the cleaning power in. The purest of the pure are mopping up with their own concoctions made with nature's own ingredients like vinegar, baking soda, borax, salt, and good old hot water. Some marketers, however, are transforming consumers' kitchens into day spas, adding plant-derived essential oils to cleaners instead of synthetic fragrances. Brands such as Method, sold at The Terrance Conran Shops, ain't your mother's cleaning product, blending Chinese ginger, gardenia, citrus, and awapuki (a Hawaiian flower) which give kitchenettes and Mr. Cleans a whiff of the rainforest while they scrub. Caldrea Green Tea Patchouli counter top cleanser and Citrus Mint Ylang Ylang dish soap are sponging off of our current obsession to make even down and dirty drudgery into an opportunity for healing. Mrs. Meyer's, Good Home, Bloom, and Indigo Wild are other biodegradable or animal-friendly brands disinfecting and deodorizing the new old-fashioned way and, for cooks who don't want their couscous to smell like Comet, Williams-Sonoma sells a piquant Basil & Lemon Verbena kitchen cleaner. Complementing all of this foaming at the mouth are all-natural turkey feather dusters, horsehair brushes, and corn brooms, which haven't been this popular since the prairie chic days of Laura Ingalls Wilder. As an affordable indulgence, natural cleaners are the very definition of good housekeeping in the 21st century and are flush with opportunity.

Go from rags to riches by making everything (including the kitchen sink!) more natural.

ARCHITECTURE: Green Homes

Gimme green shelter! That's what more of us are singing as green architecture rolls across America like a stone gathering no moss, driven by a new generation of architects who see the world through green eyes. About 3% of new buildings have some Earth-friendly features,

according to the US Green Building Council, which include geothermal heating systems, photovoltaic panels that convert sunlight into electricity, or natural air circulation for better ventilation. That number is sure to go up, however, as energy efficiency becomes a top environmental priority for builders and communities. (The power generated to supply an average home pollutes the air more than the average car because most electricity is still produced by coal-burning plants that release nitrogen oxides in their emissions and ultimately create that bad boy ozone.) In California, for example, builders are signing up for the state's voluntary Green Builders Program which encourages prudent use of natural resources and offers guidelines for energy efficiency, on-site waste recycling, and reduction of water use and air pollution. Constructing a house per the guidelines adds only $700 to $1,000 to its cost, which the happy homemaker eventually recoups in energy savings. In Richmond, Virginia, the local Habitat for Humanity recently built a green home for a low-income family to prove that environmental consciousness and economic viability are not mutually exclusive. With its double-glazed windows, high-efficiency heat pump, high-density insulation, and non-toxic paint, the joint makes your average McMansion look downright sickly. And in Cleveland, an environmentally sustainable townhouse development called EcoVillage is springing up. A national showcase for green building technologies, the solar electric powered village vividly illustrates the potential of ecologically sensitive urban life. With the National Association of Home Builders sponsoring Green Building Conferences which promote architecturally sustainable materials, products, and techniques in residential construction and land development, the green writing is on the wallboard. Builders receive incentives from local utilities when they meet Energy Star standards, a push strategy that will make consumers want to pull into green driveways. More homes like an Austin, Texas one recently featured on HGTV are undoubtedly headed to your hood soon. The home's metal roof made from recycled materials collects enough rain for drinking and laundry to make a well or the municipal water supply unnecessary, and its solar orientation maximizes breezes and minimizes heat from the Long Horn sun. Located at the intersection of financial incentive and environmental concern, green architecture suggests it's time we start cross-stitching "Home, Green Home."

Find ways to make nurturing nature a win-win situation in your product category.

TRANSPORTATION: Green Cars

Who said it ain't easy being green? Whoever did now has a frog in his throat as green cars finally become something much more than experimental curiosities. As global warming and foreign oil dependency turn the world into one big hot zone (the U.S. spends about $2 billion per week on oil imports, mostly for ozone zapping gasoline, according to the Clean Cities Coalition), green cars will soon be on cruise control. With its "Integrated Motor Assist" technology that combines gasoline and electricity, Honda's Civic Hybrid is the vehicle that's currently steering consumers down the green mile, getting upwards of 45-50 miles per gallon or 650 miles per tank. Although it would take over ten years to recover the fuel savings due to the additional cost of the car versus a regular Civic, lots of consumers are happy to help blaze the green trail. More hybrids from Toyota, Ford, Mercedes, and other car makers are racing to the marketplace, including a new generation of SUVs which will take an evolutionary leap over their fossil fuel guzzling dinosaur kin. J.D. Power found that 60% of new car buyers said they would consider a hybrid, and predicts that hybrids will own a 3% market share in a few years when 20 or so models are wandering the blue planet. Consumers are more likely to put their money where their civic-minded mouths are because of a $2,000 tax credit from the IRS and an exclusion from High Occupancy Vehicle (HOV) lane restrictions in seven states, including the parking lot that is California. Legislation, including President Bush's Freedom CAR (Cooperative Automotive Research) Initiative, is pushing auto makers to invest in green technologies, the next major one being fuel cells which release zero carbon-based emissions. The Honda FCX, the first fuel cell vehicle in the world to receive government certification, can be leased in California and Tokyo, and GM's revolutionary Hy-wire prototype utilizing hydrogen fuel cells very well could be the model of the future. Replacing steel with carbon-fiber polymers to make a lighter and more aerodynamic vehicle (as in Daimler-Chrysler's Smart Car) is another way nature will take its course in car culture. Ride shotgun as little engines that could take us up the environmentally-friendly hill.

Be the catalyst for change in your product category by shifting into green gear.

TREND COMMANDMENT 6
Nurture Nature.

KA-CHING!

AUTOS
Clean up over the long haul by making consumers think of your brand when they think of environmental friendliness.

BEAUTY
Earth to marketers! Make your products so natural consumers won't know where their bodies end and where nature begins.

ENTERTAINMENT & MEDIA
Bring the great outdoors indoors by creating a new category segment dedicated to "green entertainment."

FASHION
Rule the earth by appointing yourself the king of organic cotton and hemp.

FINANCE
Nurture a Natural Mutual Fund consisting of companies whose products are chemistry-free.

FOOD & BEVERAGE
Dig up uncommon plants from around the world to create foods and beverages that allow consumers to partake of the wonders of nature.

HEALTHCARE
Champion complementary care as Western medicine gets a warm herbal rub-down.

RETAIL
Seed a chain of stores called Green which carry and sell only natural products.

TECHNOLOGY
Ensure your gadgets and gizmos can be turned into new geegaws and thingamajigs after they become obsolete.

TRAVEL & HOSPITALITY
Devote a chunk of profits made from guiding travelers to the planet's remaining pristine environments in order to better their chances of survival.

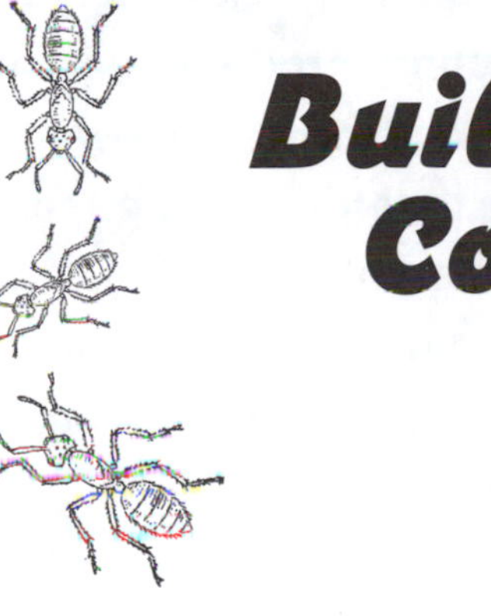

Build Community.

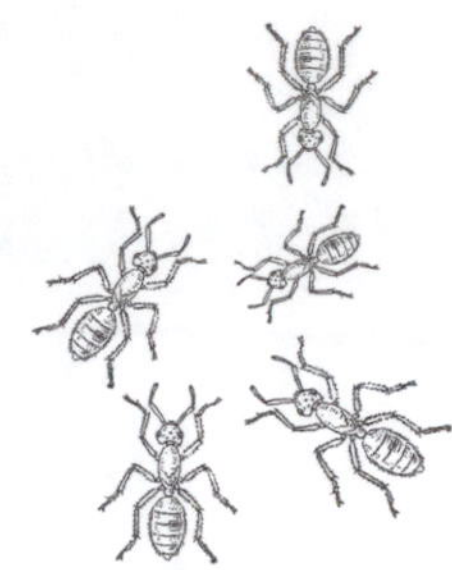

TREND COMMANDMENT 7
Build Community.

It may not be there in your job description but it should be. Marketers' real job is to create communities around their brands or, if you prefer, to turn their brands into communities. Fortunately, community is something everyone is in the market for, so to speak, especially these days when our yearning to feel connected has perhaps never been stronger. There is today a renewed celebration of public life and spirit, driving most of us to seek out communities of all kinds at the personal, local, regional, national, and global level. Traditional, non-traditional, neo-traditional, whatever-traditional communities remind us that it is relationships with other people that really matter and all the other stuff—money, success, that kicking Viking range and Sub-Zero fridge—is just icing on the flourless cake. Even if one is challenging the status quo and is a poster child for indie thought and action, one still wants to be part of a community that shares that same passion. The renaissance of community is especially amazing because on the surface it seems to run against the stream of our increasingly mobile, multicultural, MixMastered society. But it is exactly that, of course, which is making us hunger for common denominators that we can relate to, share in, and be a part of. Rather than being separate from or in opposition to our individual identities, the communities to which we choose to belong are vital ways we construct and express our personal selves.

For marketers, building communities around brands is a way to infuse them with a form of power that exceeds any particular feature or benefit they may offer. History has shown over and over the steps people will go to in the name of community, making it too valuable a marketing strategy to ignore. Consumers choose certain brands, in fact, because they believe they and the brand have something in common, that the brand is essentially a community that the consumer wants to join. The challenge for marketers is to grow their communities without diluting their power, a tricky balancing act. Here are some trends that illustrate our desire to belong to communities and some ways to go about building your own.

ARCHITECTURE:
New Urbanism

Remember when everyone knew their neighbors, walked to work, and sat on their front porches sipping homemade lemonade? Although that memory may be more Mayberry than reality, the idea is appealing enough to have spawned an architectural and design reform movement called New Urbanism. New Urbanists argue that we lost our way after World War II, when suburbia-mania put the automobile in front of people and urban renewal tore down a lot of great buildings for a lot of high-rises right out of the Eastern Europe school of architecture. More city planners are putting the brakes on the postwar American way of life, however, using the principles of New Urbanism to create what they term "complete communities" which are more pedestrian-friendly and, in theory, more socially equitable. New Urban communities call for narrow streets, wide sidewalks, alleyways, homes with porches, neighborhood squares, and bike lanes to encourage interaction and a greater sense of place. Because they are high-density, i.e., stacking home, work, school, shopping, and entertainment close together, these communities are as walkable as a Hush Puppy shoe, making people feel like they're part of a neighborhood. Other tenets include affordable housing to meet the needs of a diverse population, "human-scale" and aesthetically pleasing architecture, putting apartments over stores, and parallel street parking. On the evil list are cul-de-sacs, gated communities, parking lots and garages that can be seen from the street, and, of course, urban sprawl. Just like people, New Urbanists sensibly believe, it's important that communities have clear identities and are recognizable from each other. As well, with too many blink-and-you'll-miss-it-downtowns, New Urbanism prescribes there be a beginning, middle, and end of a town, making most of the Northeast (I-95ville) and Southern California (405land) decidedly Old Urbanism. And if this sounds like Fantasyland, think again. There are more than 500 New Urbanism developments completed or in progress in 39 states according to *New Urban News*, with such developments surging 37% a year. Downtown Baton Rouge, City Place in West Palm Beach, Harbor Town in Memphis, Crawford Square in Pittsburgh, and Park DuValle in Louisville are just a few places to subscribe to New Urbanist principles designed to take out much of the isolation and alienation from modern life ruled by the car. More city councils are gradually changing zoning laws to clear the legal way for New Urbanism, a clear sign that America has caught the community bug. As long as it steers away from *Pleasantville*, plan on New Urbanism to stay a'foot and be a path for a better quality of life.

Make your brand a vehicle that can help people bump into each other.

SPORTS:
Minor League Baseball

Once upon a time in America almost every town with a stoplight had a baseball team. Then a little thing called television happened and everyone decided to watch the big boys from their La-Z-Boys. But the story has a happy ending. Minor league baseball is now more popular than ever in its 101-year history, with attendance topping its previous high of 39 million set in 1949. That's more than half of what the majors pulls in, and is up 29% since 1993, according to *Time*. 80 minor league parks have been built in the U.S. since 1995, each one a field of dreams for fans wanting a more affordable, more intimate, and, most important, more fun experience than can be had at a big league game. Just the names of some of the 200 teams tell it all: the Lansing Lugnuts, the Rancho Cucamonga Quakes, and the San Antonio Missions, the latter cheered on by their mascot, Henry the Puffy Taco. And for $6 an average ticket (vs. $19 for the majors), fans are treated to a variety of activities far more interesting than the game itself. The Lugnuts' hot dog cannon regularly shoots wrapped wieners into the crowd, while Girl Scouts have been known to camp overnight in the Brocton (Massachusetts) Rocks' outfield. But that's peanuts compared to the promotional nights which have included the Ft. Worth Cats' "You Might Be a Redneck Night" (complete with hog calling and a pig's feet eating contest) and the Charleston River Dogs' "Two Dead Fat Guys Night" (celebrating the birthdays of the larger-than-life Babe Ruth and Elvis). The Cats have also held "Kazoo Night," "Blue Hair Night," and "Renew Your Vows Night" (a trend within a trend), while the Dogs also threw "Funeral Giveaway Night" and "Lawyer Appreciation Night," when every attorney at the game was charged twice the ticket price (the proceeds went to Legal Aid). One of the owners of the River Dogs (as well as a few other teams) is Bill Murray, who goes by the title of Director of Fun, and fellow funster Jimmy Buffett too has a piece of the action. Having a ball team in town has also helped revitalize communities such as Coney Island, whose Brooklyn Cyclones are hotter than a Nathan's hot dog on the grill. As kid-friendly family entertainment with showmanship that would make P.T. Barnum proud, minor league baseball is almost just an excuse for a local community to get together and have a good time. Watch this grassroots version of our national pastime steal home on the majors as we long to connect with each other.

Be a crackerjack marketer by building communities out of mythic Americana.

ART:
Public Art

It started with the cows. "Cows on Parade," a public art project involving 300 uniquely painted and decorated bovine, swept through Chicago like the fire from Mrs. O'Leary's barn. Soon after they were sent out to pasture, an eerily similar CowParade began grazing In New York and then mooved all around the world. Today, there's a stampeding herd of other public art installations designed to raise the profile of the host city and raise money for worthy causes by auctioning off the works. More than 300 public art programs exist in the United States at the state and local level, according to Americans for Arts' Public Art Network, each one in some way a reflection of the local community. At its best, public art is bigger than the art itself, endowing a location with a heightened sense of place and creating an opportunity to bring people together (think the Lincoln Memorial in Washington or the Statue of Liberty in New York). The invasion of artistic animalia has continued, most recently in DC where 200 plastic donkeys and elephants suddenly appeared and in Royal Oak, Michigan, which mounted a "Polar Palooza" installation featuring a number of fiberglass bears. Thankfully, not all public art is a menagerie of mannequinesque mammals. Cleveland's recent "GuitarMania," a collection of 10-foot tall replicas of Fender Stratocasters rocked, and Target's Art in the Park in New York every summer is a bullseye of how public art can get perfect strangers to talkin'. For Miami's "The Fins Project: From Swords into Plowshares," giant fins from decommissioned, Cold War-era submarines have been turned into a public monument to peace. Temporary, site-specific works of art are popping up in many cities, especially Los Angeles via its Edges and Hedges project. If you recently cruised Santa Monica Boulevard on West Hollywood, for example, you might have driven by works like Bruce Odland's "Tonic," a sound installation transforming street noise into musical harmonics in real time. 250,000 people a day took in Nam June Paik's "Transmission" and "32 cars for the 20th century: play Mozart's Requiem quietly" at Rockefeller Center last summer, and New York's springtime "Tribute of Light" memorializing the victims of 9/11 proved how powerful public art could be when done right. Count on public art to breed as more communities seek to boost civic pride, inspire creativity, and share ideas.

Support public art to corral consumers and make them eat out of your hand.

GARDENING:
Community Gardens

"Gardens are active places that people make themselves, use for work and socializing, and can 'love.'"
—Mark Francis, professor at the University of California at Davis and former board member of the American Community Gardening Association

The people have spoken. After Congress cut funding from the USDA's Urban Gardening Program at the stalks in 1993, community gardens are healthier than ever, providing positive social, economic, and environmental benefits to neighborhoods. There are some 10,000 community gardens in the United States, each one a collaborative project created and managed by local residents. Green thumbs transform empty, barren lots or junkyards into living spaces, turning urban jungles into "little islands in the madness," as a Dorchester, Massachusetts community gardener aptly put it. Versus another office or apartment building made of concrete and steel, community gardens are primal, magical oases that have an almost spiritual effect on a community. In addition to offering some peace and quiet to city folks (often more than possible in their own apartments), community gardens provide neighbors with a sense of ownership and empowerment. Developing and controlling a piece of property is inherently a political activity that strengthens community ties by exposing residents to the powers that be. And besides being a common ground that brings people together, community gardens help feed people, generate income, reduce crime and air pollution, increase property values, and provide positive health benefits (studies show that just looking at a plant lowers blood pressure and reduces muscle tension). The city of Cleveland even uses community gardening as a therapeutic activity for children from abusive environments and at-risk youths. Despite the overwhelming evidence that community gardens improve quality of life (which makes sense since they are a form of life), city or privately owned bulldozers are often waiting nearby ready to pave paradise and put up a parking lot. Many community gardens have thus banded together to form coalitions to defend Charlie Browns and their great pumpkin patches. Non-profits such as the San Francisco League of Urban Gardeners (SLUG), Denver Urban Gardens (DUG), Save Our Urban Land (SOUL) in Chicago, and the Green Guerillas™ in New York help neighborhoods organize, advocate, and, if necessary, pursue legal action against anyone who wants to squash these mini-Edens in the name of progress. Stake out community gardens as even cabbage heads recognize their power as fertile town meetings.

Dangle a carrot in front of consumers by presenting your company or brand as a thriving community.

FOOD & BEVERAGE:
Community Shared Agriculture

Now you can buy the farm without having to kick the bucket. Community shared agriculture (also called subscription farming) is where growers and consumers come together in a happy, mutually rewarding partnership, challenging the traditional buyer/seller business model. Started in Japan in the 1960s, hopping to Switzerland in 1984, and exported to New England in 1986, community shared agriculture (CSA) has shareholders "invest" in a farm's output by paying in advance for their portion of what's grown. In exchange for their annual membership fee, consumers get their share of the weekly harvest or a pre-determined amount of the goodies. There are now over 1,000 CSA programs in the United States, according to the University of Massachusetts Extension, a number growing because of the benefits they provide each party. Every week from the late spring to the early fall (year round in warmer climates), a bag of vegetables, fruit, flowers, herbs, honey, eggs, meat, or dairy foods arrives at members' doorsteps, all of which is fresher than anything at the supermarket for the same or lower cost. Farmers get to pre-sell their crops at guaranteed, fair prices, enabling many smaller growers to keep on hoeing. Less tangible but as important is the personal connection made between consumers and farmers which comprises not just a community but a kind of committed relationship. Customers get first-hand contact with the source of their food, and are encouraged to visit the farm (and preferably work it for a discount on their membership fee). Shares cost anywhere from $300 to $600, which typically feeds a family of four or a couple of veggies (half shares too are often available). CSAs are particularly exciting because they throw a big ripe tomato in the face of the long-distance relationship we have with food in the U.S., which travels an average of 1,300 miles from farm to store shelf. CSAs keep dollars close to home, generate less waste and fuel consumption because of minimal shipping, and, best of all, "puts the farmer's face on the food," as the Japanese term for subscription farming ("teikel") translates into. Watch win-win partnerships in the production, distribution, and consumption in other categories sprout via "communitarian capitalism."

Till cooperative ventures with consumers to become peas in a pod.

ONLINE:
Digital Neighborhoods

Isn't "digital neighborhoods" an oxymoron? Not really. Many neighborhoods are using virtual technology to help make their real neighborhood an even stronger and more positive force in people's lives. Just as it's become clear that the primary benefit of the Internet is not being able to order kitty litter by double-clicking on a mouse, it's become equally evident that the singular benefit of online technology all along has been (no, not 24/7 porn) but its ability to bring people together. Whether it's e-mailing grandma from your dorm room or finding the other person in the world interested in forming a Barney Rubble chat room, the Internet allows people who share something common to connect as never before. Entire neighborhoods are embracing this idea by creating websites for local citizens to strengthen their ties, an example of the Internet at its very best. Take, for example, Every Block a Village Online (EBVO), a website for westside Chicagoans. EBVO is a collaborative project that uses the Internet as a tool for community organizing, allowing block leaders to connect with their neighbors. Neighbors provide information to others on their block, teach each other new things, and become connected with other neighborhoods around the world. Westsiders are double-clicking on pages like Ask A Doc, Citizen I-CAM, Fun Things to Do, Grandparent Help Book, and the Better Business Bureau. Funded in part through a Technology Opportunity Program Grant from the U.S. Department of Commerce, EBVO is a model of digital citizenship. Many other towns and cities across the country are taking advantage of this opportunity to build healthy neighborhoods using virtual technology. Encino, California has a particularly active online community, with Valley girls and boys chatting it up over the digital fence. On the public discussion board of VenturaBlvd.com (what else?), fellow Encinoans e-schmooze about health, education, housing, and, of course, pet peeves. Recent pages included everything from someone looking for English lessons to the latest on the San Fernando Valley Teen Pageant to a collection of photos of the town's oak trees. Another dude was soliciting others to join a hackey sack webring, something which cultural anthropologists of the future will likely be very puzzled and hopefully disturbed by. Look for digital neighborhoods to continue to allow us to plug into our real communities.

Exploit the power of technology to help consumers reach out and touch someone.

RELATIONSHIPS:
E-Mentoring

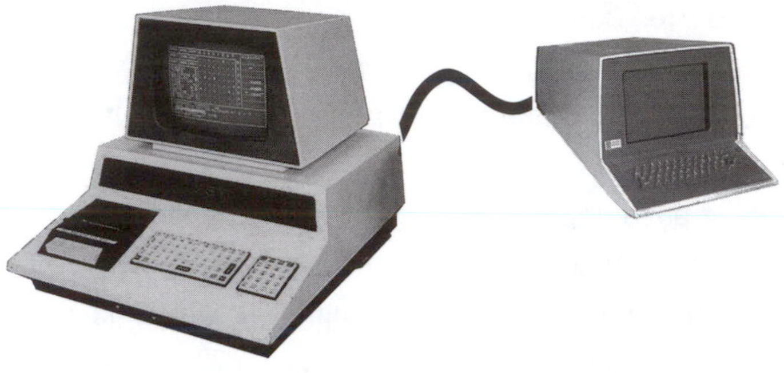

Building community happens best when it happens one-to-one. And because of the Internet, helping kids unlock their potential through mentoring is making the building of community that much easier. A number of e-mentoring programs are pairing caring adults with at-risk or underserved youths, ignoring the constraints of time and space to create a more humanitarian society one person at a time. According to AOL Time Warner, there are 15.7 million kids between 10 and 17 in the United States who could likely benefit from a mentor but only 2 million of them are currently in such a relationship. With its Mentors Online program, the you-got-mail folks are helping close that gap by making the process more convenient for everyone. The company is distributing its E-Mentoring Tool Kit™ software to partner organizations which then recruit and train employee volunteers. After matching a mentor with a mentee, the two become e-pals, the former guiding and encouraging the latter to be all that he or she can be. AOL's program builds upon another it also helped orchestrate, the Digital Heroes Campaign (DHC). Launched in 2000 and still going strong, the DHC links troubled adolescents with well-known role models ranging from athletes (e.g., Chris Evert) to zoologists (Jack Hanna). Movie stars like Matt Damon and Glenn Close too are coaching kids online at least once a week for a year, matched up with their digital friend through some common interest or background. Another program, ICouldBe.org, is an e-mentoring website that pairs at-risk students with online career mentors. The ratio of high school students to guidance counselors is 400 to 1 nationally according to Adam Aberman, the site's founder, meaning most teens are simply not getting enough information when it comes to career planning. E-mentors offer career advice to students from overcrowded urban or underserved rural schools across the U.S., helping teens set goals and providing the real skinny about the plusses and minuses of their own jobs. Expect more e-mentoring relationships to go online as graying boomers seek to pass on their been-around-the-block wisdom to kids who could use it.

Participate in e-mentoring programs to help build a healthier, happier community for all.

TRAVEL: Volunteer Vacations

"The next step [in vacations] is to do something where you want to benefit another culture."—Dan Hickey, founder of Transformational Journeys

How does hard labor, no running water, and a chance of getting malaria sound for your next vacation? More and more Americans are paying good money for exactly that, taking time off from work or school to engage in the global community through volunteer vacations. Volunteers help out on scientific, ecological, social service, and other types of projects through the help of non-profits such as Transformational Journeys, Heart to Heart International, and Volunteers for Peace which organize the humanitarian trips. Projects are scattered around the world, last anywhere from a weekend to a few months, and cost anything from just travel expenses to thousands of dollars. One can volunteer for environmental protection and research, historical restoration, marine research, health and medical services, and lots of activities involving a pick and/or shovel. Folks are headed to places like

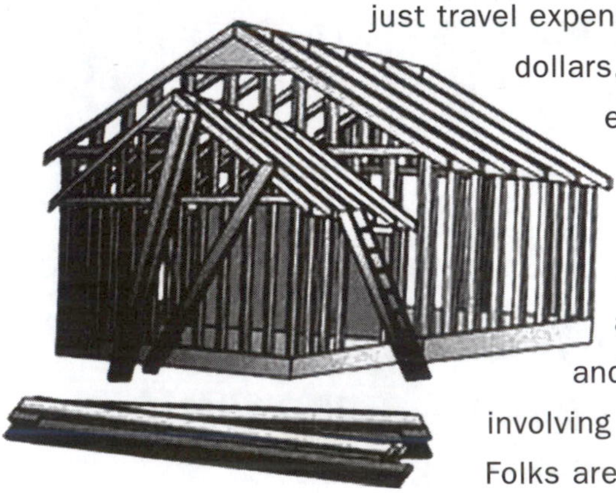

Costa Rica to document plant and animal life, Kenya to build a library, Montana to dig up dinosaur bones, and Africa to work with AIDS patients. By offering volunteer or cause vacations, nonprofit groups like the University of California Research Expeditions Program, the Earthwatch Institute, and the Oceanic Society gain vital financial resources to keep the lights on. Why are people shelling out their own bucks and giving up valuable vacation days to endure sweltering heat and sleep in mud huts when they could be sipping fruity drinks with paper umbrellas on a beach? Graduates say they get more than they give from volunteer vacations, that their experience adds new dimensions to their personality, and is an opportunity to leave a little piece of oneself on this planet before one becomes bait for a future archeologist. Such trips are also a reality check for many Americans, teaching or reminding us how much we take for granted. Originally a countercultural phenomenon, volunteer vacations have aged along with baby boomers who remain communitarians at heart. Watch more of us go from Katmandu to Timbuktu to do some good works as volunteers of America.

Put a group of your employees up at Hotel Pay It Forward.

FAMILY:
Family Reunions

"Knowing where you come from gives you a little head start on where you're going."—Edith Wagner, editor of Reunions magazine

You think getting your immediate family together for Thanksgiving or the holidays is difficult? Try getting 40 of your relatives together from all over the country in the middle of summer for a few days to celebrate the community that is your extended family. Despite requiring the logistic of a land, sea, and air military invasion, more than 200,000 American families gather for reunions every year, according to the *Christian Science Monitor*. That's 8 million people munching on chicken wings, telling stories, and engaging in as many forms of sibling revelry as there are families. Why are family reunions more popular than ever when your second cousin once removed is just an e-mail or cell phone call away? In these geographically splintered times, family reunions satisfy a basic urge to stay connected with the people that, for better or worse, crawled out of the same genetic swimming pool. Since 9/11, reunions have jumped 60%, according to the Travel Industry Association of America, ranging from an afternoon barbecue to a 72-hour and-how-exactly-are-we-related? marathon. Our increasingly mobile society has, of course, contributed to the popularity of family reunions, as formal get-togethers weren't exactly necessary when grandma lived in the basement and your in-laws lived around the corner. With relatives scattered and everyone's schedules tighter than Uncle Angus's wallet, however, planning for reunions kick in six months to a year in advance of the big event. After a family member lands a winning bid as host, committees and sub-committees are formed to orchestrate down-to-the-minute agendas, sometimes including updates on investment clubs and scholarship programs. Not surprisingly, family reunions have become a tidy little business for some marketers who recognize their power as passionate sites of community. The reunion industry is in fact a $500 million business, according to the Travel Industry Association, leading convention and visitor bureaus to hire reunion specialists. Family-Reunion.com is the granddaddy of reunion websites, offering software to make the Olympian task a bit easier, and MyFamily.com can create a private website that family members can access 24/7. Well aware of the special role that reunions play for African Americans (accounting for 45% of their non-business travel!), *Ebony* recently sent a Black Family Reunion Tour Truck to 10 cities, allowing sponsors like Procter & Gamble to participate in families' pride, achievement, and joy. Expect family reunions to be fruitful and multiply as we celebrate communities of kinship.

Think of other ways to get families to reconnect and share the love.

CRAFTS:
Knitting Circles

Better watch your back, granny. A new generation of knitters from Adelaide to Yazoo City is adopting the communal mantra of "knit-one-purl-two." Like quilting bees, knitting circles offer members a safe, supportive environment in which to socialize while creating something original and functional. Young, urban, sophisticated knitwits (often groups of friends or co-workers) are flocking to these wild and wooly gatherings and walking away more relaxed, less stressed out, and carrying a handmade sweater, scarf, or baby outfit. A new knitter joins the ranks every minute in America, according to the Craft Yarn Council of America, which also found that 38 million American women (one in four) know how to knit or crochet. While knitting circles are primarily a chick thing, the occasional stray male does indeed drop in to dish the dirt and chat it up about life on the outside. Although knitting circles serve as social anchors where members can confide in each other, these stitch-and-bitch session ain't just about gossip. Yarnaholics report a "knitter's high" from the rhythmic activity and the losing track of time as they focus on the tactile task in hand.

Medical research bears out the therapeutic nature of knitting, with clear evidence showing that working with needles and thread often lowers one's blood pressure and heart rate. (Cancer patients especially are finding it contributes to the healing process.) The meditative, Zen-like state associated with knitting has led enthusiasts to call it "the new yoga" (although bikram knitting in 100 degree heat has thankfully yet to turn up as a trend). Some of Hollywood's biggest stars are regular knitters, filling the time in-between scenes while on set or dropping in at La Knitterie Parisienne, a boutique in Studio City, to mix it up with other actors, agents, directors, and producers. Julia Roberts, Cameron Diaz, Uma Thurman, and Daryl Hannah are all confirmed knitters, as is, rather surprisingly, gladiator Russell Crowe. Celebrities often auction off their knitted and crocheted handbags or blankies on ebay with the proceeds going to various good causes. Teens and kids too are learning the craft, ensuring that knitting is something that will probably grow like the proverbial never-ending scarf in the years ahead. With *Vogue Knitting* recently adding "Teen Knits" to its "On the Go" series of instructional books, should we start referring to Generation Y as "Generation Yarn"?

Spin some marketing magic by making your product or service a bonding experience.

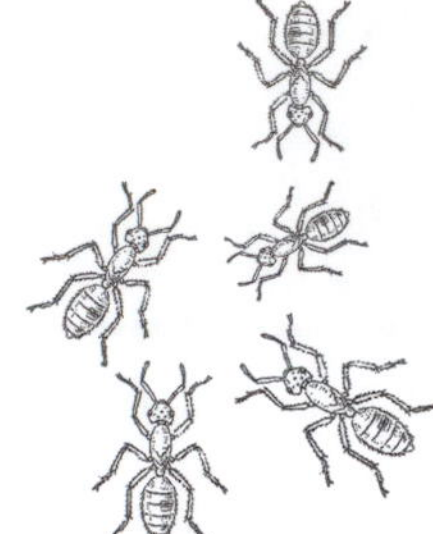

TREND COMMANDMENT 7
Build Community.

KA-CHING!

AUTOS
Present being in your vehicles as being part of a community of family or friends.

BEAUTY
Create a community for consumers to swap beauty secrets online.

ENTERTAINMENT & MEDIA
Leak news about upcoming projects into chat rooms dedicated to your artists to jumpstart the publicity machine.

FASHION
Weave your brands into the fabric of community life by sponsoring public art.

FINANCE
Earn big dividends by investing in community gardens, mentoring programs, and volunteer vacations.

FOOD & BEVERAGE

Sip from the communal bowl by making your brand the official product of local, regional, national, and global festivals.

HEALTHCARE

Appoint yourself Dr. Feelgood by tending to the health of a whole community versus individual patients.

RETAIL

Be inclusive versus exclusive by viewing your store not just for a specific group of shoppers but as a community destination.

TECHNOLOGY

Define your mission as to bring people together via your product or service.

TRAVEL & HOSPITALITY

Present traveling and your brand as an opportunity to become an honorary member of other communities.

TREND 8 COMMANDMENT

Surf the Edge.

TREND COMMANDMENT 8
Surf the Edge.

Surf's up, dude! Better grab your board because it's in the shallow waters right off the cultural mainland where many trends tend to float like flotsam and jetsam. Do not confuse the edge, however, with cool. The edge can surf rings around cool, not concerned with what people think, how it looks, what kind of shoes it wears. Edge culture is willing to take risks, look foolish, face social ostracism. It's about pushing the envelope at both the individual and cultural level, in it for the passion versus the money or the image. Edge tends to be non-linear, non-rational, non-Western, open to things and ideas that can't be touched or seen. Importantly, the edge is more a state of mind or way of life than a particular group of people. We all have some edge in us, yes, even you, the guy with more pairs of Dockers than J.C. Penny. Still, edge tends to skew towards sub-cultures —youth, gays, minorities, New Agers—as it is these groups who've been cast to the periphery of society and cut off from traditional economic and political power. Instead, sub-cultures wield a much different and perhaps even more influential form of power, largely dictating popular tastes for the rest of us. Extreme sports came directly from youth culture, for example, body art and Ecstasy from gay culture, guayaberas from Latinos, and yoga and aromatherapy from New Agers. Wall Street may rule the financial world and Washington the governmental arena, but when it comes to clothes, music, food, and just about everything else, look to the margins.

For marketers, surfing the edge means allowing the margins to seep into your corporate culture, brands, and plans. Look to sites of edge culture and think of ways to incorporate their essence into your products and services. Before you know it, you'll be barreling, tubing, and tailsliding like Blue Crush. Aren't you stoked?

SPORTS:
Adventure Racing

What's a boy or girl to do after finishing a marathon and then a triathlon? Always looking for the next mountain to climb and stream to fjord, more type-A athletes are embracing the multi-sport challenge of adventure racing. The sport makes standing on that surf-, snow-, or skateboard seem downright wimpy, putting physical endurance ahead of the fancy schmancy tricks of other extreme sports. Adventure racing is growing by literal leaps and bounds, climbing from 50 races a couple of years ago to over 300 today. Racers in 2-5 person teams mountain bike, hike, canoe, kayak, "hydro-speed" (whitewater swim), and/or rappel for a few hours to over a week in both exotic and urban locations. Top races are in places like Borneo, New Zealand, Brazil, China, and Tibet, offering racers a view of the world unavailable to the usual tourist. The mother of all adventure races is the Iditasport in Alaska, a 350-mile running, biking, and cross-country-skiing trek normally covered by sled dogs. In urban adventure races such as Chicago's 24-hour "Wild Onion," teams scale buildings and snake through busy intersections, not knowing the actual route until two hours before start-time. 15% of participants reportedly don't finish one-day adventure races, while three-fourths drop out of longer ones. With just finishing considered a victory in adventure racing, what's the big appeal? Adventure racers are drawn by the opportunity to stretch one's perceived limits, to discover that one can do more than one had thought if necessary. Egos are checked at the door, as that fat job or comfort that Oprah will take your calls ain't going to help you get over the river and through the woods any easier. Many of the best adventure racers are in their late-30s to mid-40s, people who want to prove to themselves that they haven't gone soft even though they're a desk monkey and drive a minivan. One outfit, Odyssey Adventure Racing, has seized the adventurous day by offering "Corporate Challenges" to company men and women. Run by ex-Navy SEALS and ex-U.S. Special Forces officers (yikes!), these races are designed to build teamwork, instill leadership, encourage risk-taking and decision-making, and get executives to think out of their corporate box. A team from Daimler-Chrysler, in fact, felt that "this was something we will remember for the rest of our lives." Odyssey promises that less fit managers will not be left behind to be eaten by a pack of wolves. Adventure racing is the Powerade of sports, fueled by testosterone and a desire to prove one's physical and mental toughness.

Explore high performance products and services for folks who approach life as an adventure.

TRAVEL:
Monastery Retreats

"Be not forgetful to entertain strangers: for thereby some have entertained angels unawares." —Hebrews 13:1-2

Oh brother, where art thou? Perhaps at one of the thousands of monasteries around the world that welcomes visitors. For the last 1,600 years or so, travelling monks have been checking in at monasteries as a respite from their long pilgrimages. This tradition of Christian monasticism continues today as these refuges from the modern world open their big wooden doors to increasing numbers of 21st century pilgrims seeking spiritual renewal, soulful reflection, or just some peace and quiet. Monks have, of course, renounced their self-will and pursuit of material goods, having taken vows of poverty, chastity, and obedience. Their "cenobetic" (literally, "common") way of life means that except for the abbot, it's all for one and one for all, with monks eating together, working together, and keeping the same daily schedule. This kind of community living, monks believe, offers a deeper vision of humanity than life on the outside, a pious and pure experience conducive to unselfish love and compassion. With such ideals, it's not surprising that material girls and boys want to witness or participate in monastery life, perhaps in the hope that some of the sacredness will rub off on our profane ways. One can join the chorus of Byzantine chant at the chapel services of St. Theodore House, for example, a Greek Orthodox monastery in Galion, Ohio, or follow the daily prayer cycle at the Heritage of the Holy Cross in upstate New York. Better set your alarm early, though, because liturgies start promptly at 3 a.m.. Following the good book's rule to "support themselves by the labor of their hands," most monasteries produce and sell goods such as icons, ceramics, wovens, calligraphics, and hand-rolled incense. The Holy Brotherhood of the Monastery of the All-Merciful Savior on the Island of Vashon in Puget Sound not only sells prayer ropes but their own lines of gourmet "Monastery Blend" coffees and "Orthodox Monk's" teas (whadja expect, it's just a 20 minute ferry ride from Seattle). Asian monasteries such as the Jikji Temple in South Korea are also attracting visitors seeking an intensive meditative experience (no electronics allowed), and convents too, like the Monasterio de San Benito de Montserrat (an hour outside Barcelona, Spain) are becoming a popular habit among more adventurous travelers. Count on this truly orthodox trend to gain converts.

Take communion with consumers by offering total sanctuary from stress.

ARCHITECTURE:
Vastu Shastra

Which direction does your head face when you sleep? If it's north or east, you're in luck, as that's consistent with the principles of vastu shastra, the ancient Indian practice of home design and decorating. Literally "abode knowledge" in Hindu, vastu shastra (also called Sthapatya Ved) dates back to the 10th century, passed on through Sanskrit texts. Like Chinese feng shui, vastu shastra holds that furniture placement is key to creating positive energy in a building and warding off bad vibes. But vastu shasta goes much further, offering a system by which to design a home, workplace, or even whole community that is consistent with the laws of the universe. Companies like Architectural Design Services and Serene Interiors are creating living spaces designed in cosmic order, spreading the idea that a building is much more than a box with four walls. The basic concept is that living spaces have specific regions that are ruled by different deities and magnetic fields, with vastru shastra a way to bridge man and nature or establish a relationship among the dweller, the dwelling, and the universe. Because of the location of the five deities (Fire, Water, Earth, Space, and Air) in the cosmos, which rooms to put where in a residential or commercial building is vital. Since Agni, the ruler of fire, dwells in the southeast part of the cosmos, for example, one should try to put the kitchen in the southeast part of one's house. Put a deity in a room he or she doesn't feel comfortable in and you run the risk of creating an environment in which anxiety, stress, depression, and sickness can breed (just like the time you let your friend crash on your sofa for three months). Designing and decorating your building in accordance with the laws of nature, on the other hand, will generate a climate of comfort, bliss, calmness, and fulfillment. Just as a car's balance is thrown off if one of the tires is under inflated, a vastru shastra practitioner would say, it's critical to ensure that a house or workplace is properly balanced lest allow misfortune in the door. Good vibes are most likely to happen, in other words, when architecture and interior design are in holistic sync with nature. Although vastu shastra runs contrary to the West's right-brain rule that seeing is believing, it's not much of a leap to make that people are indeed influenced by the spaces in which they live and work. Look for a greater desire among many to live in harmony with the larger forces at work.

Capitalize on Americans' faith in believing things that they can't truly understand.

FASHION: Urban Apparel

Feeling a bit phat? More people are as the Hip-Hop Economy hops around the world like the celebrated jumping frog from Calaveras County. As P. Diddy and others put some soul into the *schmata* trade, urban apparel is taking Seventh Avenue by storm. The urban apparel market is now a $58 billion a year business, according to NPD Fashion World, and is forecasted to grow another 50% by 2007. As more 14 to 30 year olds look to urban apparel to dress for success, stores such as Bloomingdales and Macy's are giving premium shelf space to brands like Sean Jean, Enyce, Triple 5 Soul, Rocawear, and FUBU. Bringing entertainment to fashion is the heart and soul of urban apparel, as hip-hop culture exploits clothing's role as a form of performance. Like P. Diddy, whose Sean John apparel arm of his Bad Boy Entertainment empire brought in $250 million last year, rappers like Jay-Z, Snoop Dogg, and Outkast have launched their own clothing lines. With its Wu Wear line, the Wu Tang Clan has become a playa in the rag trade, selling Wu Shoes, Wu Pants, Wu Shirts, and Wu Jackets (whew!). Triple 5 Soul hit it big when MTV VJs and artists like De La Soul and A Tribe Called Quest started wearing the company's tie-top hats in the early 1990s.

Today you can find the Triple 5 Soul in Sweden, Germany, and Japan, where the company has stores in Osaka and Shibuya. Brands like Enyce and Phat Farm have also become icons of the street, while FUBU ("For Us, By Us") offers everything from their trademark rugby shirts and hockey shirts to tuxedos. MeccaUSA wears its multicultural roots on its sleeve, claiming that "diversity is ingrained in our crosshairs," while School of Hard Knocks emanated not from a salon in Paris or Milan but an apartment in Queens. With urban apparel playing polo with the likes of Ralph and Tommy, other marketers are looking to hip-hop culture to help kick it in their own category. To help launch Rbk, its street-inspired clothing and shoe brand, for example, Reebok International has been throwing a series of "Sounds & Rhythms of Sport" parties where athletes like Lennox Lewis and musicians like P. Diddy and Jay-Z can collectively hip and hop. The company is also teaming athletes with musicians in its advertising, using the powerful language of hip-hop to sew up mainstream fashion sensibilities. Take a walk down the urban apparel street to find out what's headed to Main Street.

Put some soul into your brands to phatten up your bottom line.

PETS:
Pet Resorts

Does your pet get bored when he's board? Now dogs and cats can have as good a time as their away-from-home owners at resorts and spas catering to the canine and feline set. More kennels, animal hospitals, and veterinary clinics are repositioning themselves as luxury hotels for pets, appealing to owners' desire for the shorter, furrier members of their family to also live full lives. There are 135 million pets at more than one out of every two households in the United States according to the Pet Food Institute, creating what the American Boarding Kennels Association estimates to be a $1.5 billion pet boarding market. And with the kind of accommodations and amenities available for doggies and kitties, one begins to wonder who's on which side of the evolutionary fence. In their chauffeured van on the way over to the Bark Avenue Pet Resort in Hollywood, Florida, for example, guests are treated to movies such as *Lady and the Tramp* and *101 Dalmatians*. During their stay at Bark Avenue, dogs drink filtered water, get scrubbed with natural soap, and sleep on animal-print linens. Guests are supervised while they play (matched up with friends of a similar size), and hammocks and couches are provided for pooch potatoes. Massage and acupuncture too are available for pets with those post-workout aches and pains. Down the road at the South Beach Animal Hospital, pets get to watch cable TV in deluxe rooms like the Rock 'n Roll Suite and Safari Suite, with night lights offered to 'fraidy cats. At the Tail End Pet Resort and Spa in Davie, Florida, dogs sip Bark-A-Cino (made with soy milk) and nibble on three-cheese pizzas delivered by room service. Cats got it even better, plopped directly in view of a 44-gallon fish tank and cockatiel. Evening classes ("puppy kindergarten") are available to dogs wanting to learn a few new tricks. Finally, at the Paradise Ranch Country Club for Dogs in Sun Valley, California, an extra $5 gets a staff member to sleep in the same bed as that homesick hound. Although pets may not know the difference between a five star resort and a fleabag motel, the one paying the bill sure does, enough reason to make vacations for pets something to chew on.

Create your own pet projects and watch consumers bite.

RELATIONSHIPS: Tribes

Tracking the sometimes outside-the-lines steps of youth culture is a prime way to learn a lot about the general state of the state. And for a growing number of kids around the world, "tribes" are serving as an alternative, under-the-radar community that tell us lots about the cracks in our social foundation. As *The New York Times* reported in June 2002, tribes are multi-ethnic, multi-racial groups of teens and younger 20-somethings with their own cultural codes, rituals, language, politics, and music. These extended, heterogeneous sub-cultures date back to the early 1990s, when British ravers disenchanted with the overcommercialized, pretentious scene dropped out to create their own scene. Today tribes are a buzzing hive of youth culture, surrogate families for kids who are disenfranchised and disconnected from their immediate family, school, or religious institution. Although led by "tribal elders," the groups make decisions democratically, and charge no membership fees. The primary mission of tribes is simply to throw parties, usually in rented out spaces in basements, warehouses, or abandoned buildings. For about a $10 cover, some 100 tribe members dance, schmooze, play Twister, and do the occasional drug (Ecstasy and Special K are the chemicals du jour, but the high-energy drink Red Bull is the stimulant of choice).

Pierced in every place imaginable (and some unimaginable) and decked out in streetwear, tribalists groove to DJs spinning electronica, techno, trance, drum and bass, and jungle. The parties serve not only as social gatherings but also as safe havens from often mean urban streets. Tribes occasionally make field trips to museums or road trips to other cities to meet other tribes, with some groups actually owning school buses to get around. Most tribes, such as PLUR (Peace, Love, Unity, Respect) are indeed peaceful, sharing a philosophy not unlike the trippy idealists of the counter-culture. The very existence of tribes signals the dire need for places for teens to get together, and that youth culture will form their own marginal communities when traditional ones fail them. As Generations Y and Z continue to splinter and fragment in a gazillion subcultures, look for tribes of all stripes to put down stakes.

Seat your brand within leading edge youth culture by sponsoring safe, drug-free places for teens to gather.

MUSIC:
Outsider Music

What kinds of music do people who've heard it all before listen to? Good chance it's music never intended to be heard by a large, commercial audience. "Outsider music" is getting louder and louder as more listeners

head into the margins to escape today's overproduced, pitch-perfect pop. Like its marginal cousin, outsider art, outsider music is created by the self-taught who reside well outside the outskirts of the professional artistic community. Outsider music can most likely be found in the el cheapo bins of thrift stores or, increasingly, on the Internet where fans swap the latest finds. The technology is decidedly lo-fi, often recorded on reel-to-reel tape decks in homes or garages. Check out, for example, the Skaggs 1969 recording *Philosophy of the World* and hear three sisters from New Hampshire warble in a way never to be heard on "TRL." Or *The Langley Sisters Music Project: Innocence and Despair,* a circa-1970s album recorded by a music teacher in a gym. Hearing a bunch of Canadian schoolchildren sing Fleetwood Mac's "Rhiannon" or David Bowie's "Space Oddity" is guaranteed to give you shivers with its surreal and disturbing sound. The recording is a huge smash on the underground music scene, prompting Hollywood to plan on making a movie based on it. Braver souls may want to track down one of Jandek's 28 albums (which include such joyfests as *White Box Requiem*, *Blue Corpse*, *Twelfth Apostle*, and *Graven Image*) to hear some of the most desolate and structureless pieces of work this side of Samuel Beckett. The beauty of outsider music is its genuineness, naivete, pre-ironic sincerity which shine through its undeniable incompetence and ineptitude. Listen to a recording by people like B.J. Snowden, Wesley Wills, Hasil Adkins, or H.P. Lovecraft and enter an alternative universe that is undoubtedly flawed but even more original and spontaneous. The musicians themselves—surprise, surprise—are often like characters in a Tom Waits song—eccentric, sanity-challenged, and loners who definitely march to the beat of a different drum. Small labels like Arf! Arf! Records are jumping on the demand for this anti-Muzak, giving more of us the chance to explore the uncharted terrain of this kind of music which trades slickness for freshness.

Listen up to consumers' desire for the rough, the raw, and the real.

RADIO:
Alt-Radio

"Don't hate the media, become the media."
—Jello Biafra

In today's homogenized, pasteurized, corporatized audio landscape, you got to head to the literal margins of the radio dial to hear the sounds of tomorrow. The Telecommunications Act of 1996 allowed just a few media companies like Clear Channel, Infinity, and Citadel to gobble up almost half of the country's 10,000 radio stations and beam hundreds of thousand watts of middle-of-the-road programming to the masses' ears. But take a louie into the lower netherworld of the radio spectrum and you'll hear the sounds of diversity. College stations especially are faint but vibrant voices in the radio wilderness, a direct pipeline into the alternative world of progressive youth culture. In the New York City area, for example, check out WFDU-FM (89.1) on Friday mornings to hear what's coming 'round the mountain in the bluegrass scene or WFUV (90.7) on Saturday afternoons to hear a student-produced and -hosted sports show that "substitutes fun and fanaticism for the slickness found on the big networks." Such stations are committed to presenting a wide variety of

information and music outside the commercial, mass-marketed machine, often serving as clear-as-a-bell sirens of what's next. A full-fledged grassroots radio movement is also out there in the ether, consisting of folks who fight for the right for the medium to give low power to the people in an ever-narrowing, continually consolidating environment. But as the lines between radio and the Internet get increasingly fuzzy, there is more opportunity than ever to pick up a strong signal of what's going on in the margins. Dial up 3wk.com, for example, an Internet-only alternative radio station which delivers on their promise of "independent, underground, and intensely satisfying" and their mission of "Eating Bandwidth All Over the Planet." A great online radio station is the aptly named BraveNewWorld.net hosted by Tricia Halloran which streams her L.A.-based KCRW-FM show live and offers lots of monthly CD recommendations (along with links to official band sites). Expect the Web to fulfill radio's original charter to be a voice of the people.

Listen in on old media and new media alternative radio stations to get an earful of audible passion.

LITERATURE :
Comic Books & Graphic Novels

Where should you head faster than a speeding bullet to get an early read on what's trickling in from the literary margins? Comic books and graphic novels, long a voice of society's fringe, are on the rebound as a new generation of writers, artists, and marketers capture the hot zones of our daily planet. After going due south in the 1990s as costs rose and distributors and retailers shrank, the comic book industry is experiencing a renaissance buoyed, of course, by Hollywood-licensed blockbuster films. Marvel and DC remain the super heroes of the business with a combined 60% market share, and are more often exploring social issues like the sexual identity of lead character Terry Berg in *Green Lantern*. But it is the smaller publishers who are creating the truly marvelous stuff, literally illustrating that the art form is much more than disposable, adolescent fluff. Hit your nearest comic book specialty store or, better yet, attend one of the industry's conventions or the annual Alternative Press Expo and you're in for an otherworldly experience. Underground comic books like *Love and Rockets* and *Too Much Coffee Man* are smart, edgy, and high-brow, a much different animal than your mainstream guy-in-spandex-tights-chasing-after-evil-doer deal. Classic readers of alternative comiczines are no Jugheads, most often nerdy intellectuals who often cross over into the neo-punk music scene. Graphic novels, which are self-contained (vs. serialized) and often hundreds of pages long, are also gaining fans as they penetrate the shell of society with their sharp, sarcastic, and satirical take on the zeitgeist. Although they remain much more appreciated in Japan and Europe than in the States, graphic novels are up, way up, especially on Hollywood's radar. Daniel Clowe's graphic novel *Ghost World* was turned into a successful film, making other movie and television execs scurry to comic book conferences to discover the next big thing. Perhaps the most exciting news is the digitalization of comic books as they are launched online by savvy entrepreneurs. CrossGeneration Comics is leading the comic book charge on the Web, offering no less than 13 titles spread across eight genres (including sci-fi, mystery, historical fantasy, and my favorite, Samurai epic). For just $1 a month (!) subscription fee, readers get an interactive experience delivered in, appropriately enough, Flash technology (go to the Algelfire or Tripod portals at Lycos.com). Always an open window revealing central themes in American culture (heroism in the Depression, patriotism in World War II, science fiction in the Atomic Age, and politics in the late '60s), comic books are a breath of fresh air worth sucking in.

Feast on our insatiable appetite for storytelling as a cultural anchor.

SEX:
Sex Workshops

Do you know your S.Q. (Sex Quotient)? We spend years in school learning about cosines and pluperfects but when it comes to *it*, we usually let nature take its course. Letting Mother Nature be the dominatrix of one's sex life is changing, however, as more of us take classes in the do's and don'ts of doing it. Old and not-so old dogs are learning new tricks at sexual workshops being held at different forums. A popular class at The Learning Annex, for example, is "The Art of Seduction and Erotic Talk," where lovers learn how to whisper (or shout) not-so-sweet somethings into their partners' ears. Retailers too are jumping into bed, seduced by what is a $500 million market in North America for sex toys, according to Rebecca Rosenblatt, a.k.a. Dr. Date, a Toronto radio personality. At the shops Good for Her and Come As You Are in that city, instructors offer classes called "Techniques in Foreplay," "Erotic Spanking," and "Sensual Discipline." Every $30 seat is typically filled with students eager to learn things like the finer points of what to do with a man's, well, finer point. Women significantly outnumber men, who seemingly would rather ask for driving directions than inquire where one should turn or park on a woman's body. With sexuality making the moves on the public discourse via television (*Sex and the City*), theater ("The Vagina Monologues"), and, of course, online porn, America is finally shedding its

Puritanical shame when it comes to the hotter and heavier side of life. Other factors—greater monogamy in our safe-sex society, aging boomers' commitment to use it lest they lose it, and the growing popularity of Eastern techniques like tantra and the Kama Sutra—are also contributing to the overall sexualization of our culture. Sex has not surprisingly checked in at various leading spas like Canyon Ranch in Tucson, where one can get consultations in the subject and hear lectures with titles like "Sex: Body and Soul." The Oaks at Ojai in California teaches a class called "Sexuality Secrets," while Mii Amo Resort in Sedona offers a four-night "Conscious Loving" package for about $4,000 a couple, rubber props included (would that be the Continental plan?). Folks visiting the Surf and Sand Resort in Laguna Beach are also learning how to increase their strokes in the bedroom versus how to lower them on the golf course. Watch our love affair with sex to get even steamier as it becomes seen as part and parcel of our physical, emotional, and spiritual well-being.

Get in bed with sexuality to satisfy consumers' lust for love, American style.

TREND COMMANDMENT 8
Surf the Edge.

KA-CHING!

AUTOS
Go where no man (or woman) has gone before by driving design and engineering into no man's (or woman's) land.

BEAUTY
Surf the edge of beauty to ride a wave of popularity.

ENTERTAINMENT & MEDIA
Make a splash with youth sub-cultures to get the buzz trickling.

FASHION
Take a good look at the fringe of fashion before sewing up your next big deal.

FINANCE
Put your money in investment opportunities that throw a monkey wrench into business as usual.

FOOD & BEVERAGE

Nibble on the margins to
inspire your next main course.

HEALTHCARE

Investigate therapies outside
the right brain of Western medicine.

RETAIL

Head down the side streets of retail to
differentiate yourself from everyone else.

TECHNOLOGY

Hire the geekiest of geeks to see
a sky of an entirely different color.

TRAVEL & HOSPITALITY

Camp out on the frontier of tourism
to get an edge on the competition.

MARRAKECH
HAWAII
MENTON
SANTA CATALINA
DEUTSCHE
THE ORIENTAL HOTEL LTD
KOBE
HOTEL
MAMOUN
MEXICALI
NAIRO
KENYA
RAFFLES HOTEL
SINGAPORE
HOTEL MA
IC
KUALA LUMPUR
MALAYA
NEW YORK
MINERVA
FIRENZE
ISTHM
FLORI
HOTEL

TREND COMMANDMENT 9

Think (and Act) Global.

TREND COMMANDMENT 9
Think (and Act) Global.

Is it me or does the world feel like a cotton sweater that you put in the dryer even though it said, "Dry Clean Only"? Planet Earth, which seemed like a size XL not too long ago, is more like a petite these days as the geographic and cultural fabric of our lives shrinks and contracts. Thinking globally and acting locally may have been a sound philosophy as recently as a decade ago but now such an idea is untenable if not plain impossible. With the end of the Cold War and rise of a communications medium that makes having an intimate relationship with someone in Taipei or Sydney an everyday affair, it's only natural that one should not only think global but act global. America has, of course, always been a multicultural nation, our special, unique experiment in creating one society out of many cultures ("e pluribus unum") the thing that differentiates us from every other civilization, past and present. But now something equally revolutionary is brewing as apple pie America seems to more resemble a kung pao chimichanga.

With the strip-malling of sushi and yoga, Telemundoing of television, and highest immigration levels of Asians and Hispanics in history, the United States has become the fusion food on the world's buffet line. Fear and ignorance will unfortunately forever keep us all from being one big happy family, but the stuff of everyday life—food, music, clothing, etc.—always has a way of seeping through the cultural cracks and winning the day over separatism and isolationism. In short, the 20th century was very much the American Century, but the 21st century already is the Global Century.

For marketers, thinking and acting globally could be the most exciting thing since Ted Bates's U.S.P.. Many of the most interesting, dynamic, and opportunistic ideas and things are where disparate cultures intersect, creating synergistic hybrids that never existed before. Just as in nature, where cross-breeding and -pollination often result in the healthiest, most disease-resistant organisms, conceiving business opportunities by getting a Capulet and a Montague (or a Jet and a Shark) in bed together usually creates some mighty interesting sparks. Here are a few ways America is sleeping around with multiple cultures to get you in the mood.

MUSIC:
World Beat

With classical music about two centuries post-peak and pop music having lost much of its pop, is there any hope for music? There is indeed as native and Western musics swirl into a cacophonous fusion of what is collectively called world beat. Imported and exported from every place imaginable, world beat is well on the way to becoming the soundtrack to our lives, a pan-aural backdrop to the new world disorder. The ability to download music from the Internet has thrown the seeds of music into the air where they are cross-pollinating and taking root as global sonic purees like Afrocelt, Congapunk, bossa nova hip hop, and Indian electronica, complete with sitar. The huge number of immigrants in this country is another factor driving the popularity of world beat in the States, as new Americans tweak the trajectory of popular culture as they always have. For a break from the standard American fare of pubescent pop and country twang, check out for instance Los De Abajo, who mixes ska, funk, and mariachi, or the Nortec Collective, who makes a merengue out of techno and Mexican norteno. Or go around the world in 80 minutes and hear how our all-access culture has us dancin' in the streets via Azucar Negra, who combines samba, ragga, hip hop, and samba, or Cui Jian, who adds Chinese zithers to punk, jazz, and Afrobeat. For over a decade now, ex-Talking Head's David Byrne's Luaka Bop label has been a champion of world beat, rounding up a diverse array of artists who are on the A-list of music aficionados. Luaka Bop (don't ask what it means as the story continually changes) offers music from artists such as Susana Baca ("the voice of black Peru"), Bloque ("psychotropical funk from Columbia"), Paula Braganca ("Portugal's punk fadista"), Los Amigos Invisibles ("Venezuelan pop and bump 'n grind"), Os Mutantes ("samba/pop mutants"), Jim White (trip folk Americana"), Tom Ze' ("Brazilian dada pop"), and King Chango ("house band of the urban planet"). As the musical equivalent to fusion food, world beat shows a total disregard for maps, leading the way towards an increasingly borderless future. Count on our audible landscape to further melt and meld into a global soup.

Turn other forms of global culture into products and services which cross borders without a passport.

FASHION:
Soccer Jerseys

It may be taking a bit longer than originally thought for soccer to become the next big American spectator sport but soccer fashion has already reached a fever pitch. With every match of the 2002 World Cup televised in the States for the first time and the American's great showing, official and replica versions of the team's jersey have been flying off store shelves. Counterfeiters are knocking off Nike's Cool Motion Jersey, a sure sign that soccer fashion has entered the lexicon of our pop culture vocabulary. The shirt, which lists at $89.99, took years to develop, incorporating a Dri-Fit inner layer and "hydrophobic" outer layer which "thermo-insulates" as the player (or wearer) moves. Nike makes uniforms for seven other World Cup teams, which no doubt has contributed to the jump in its soccer division business from sales of $40 million in 1994 to over $500 miilion today. But the U.S. jersey is not the only one much sought after as more men leave their t-shirts and button-downs in their dresser drawers and closets. Soccer jerseys are redesigned for participating countries each World Cup, creating a four-year cycle of football fashion mania that, on a global level, makes our presidential election campaign seem like a major yawn. Fellows and some gals can be seen sporting Argentinean, Ecuadorian, and Mexican jerseys in larger American cities, reflecting Latinos' enthusiasm, to put it mildly, for all things soccer. When the wait staff at Bar Pitti, a popular restaurant in Greenwich Village, wore Italian soccer jerseys flown in from Florence, customers clamored to buy the shirts right off the servers' backs. Fortunately, jersey marketers make their products a bit easier to be had. At Adidas.com, one can find the French team's jersey, a 100% ClimaLite shirt with rib-knit collar, embroidered badge, and mesh sides for breathability. England's reversible jersey (red side for competition, blue side for fun), available from Umbro, includes a 2-way reflective loop label and a holographic logo guaranteeing authenticity. And at Puma.com, one may purchase Cameroon's bold sleeveless jersey that was promoted, by the way, with an anime print and television advertising campaign. Watch soccer jerseys to one day rival the ubiquitous backwards baseball cap as a symbol of team pride.

Make it your goal to create a coat of many colors in your category.

SMOKING:
Hookahs

Now that the stogie has thankfully been snuffed out, Americans are lighting up international style. Hookah lounges are opening up from South Beach to Seal Beach, a swanky repackaging of something enjoyed by working class Middle Easterners, Africans, and Asians for centuries. Like the Caterpillar in *Alice in Wonderland*, patrons puff on Turkish water pipes, taking in the mild, fragrant smoke as a hedonistic pleasure and affordable indulgence. Here in the States the hookah experience is quite a different animal, recast as a highly sensory, communal get-together often in exotic surroundings intended to invoke another place. At the Hookah Den in Boston's Mantra restaurant or the MGM Grand in Las Vegas, for example, guests can choose from dozens of fruity flavors of tobacco for about $20 a bowl, almost 100 times the cost of your average smoke in downtown Cairo. At the Giza Lounge in San Jose, customers sit on velvet covered couches and colorful Egyptian pillows while hooked up to nine hookahs, each of them sporting two or three hoses. Flavor choices include apple, strawberry, mint, and jasmine, with each 20-30 minute serving costing $14.95 (standard) or $19.95 (premium). No alcohol is served at the Giza Lounge, making it a destination of choice for 18 to 20 year olds who are desperate for places to meet. And at Up 'N Smoke in Moreno Valley, California (another place exempted from that state's no smoking ban), guests get to mix their own CDs, creating their personalized, customized sensory environment. Best of all, the air in hookah lounges is surprisingly non-smoky, much less so in fact than that in your typical cigarette-infused bar. Another plus is that hookah tobacco contains less than 1% nicotine, no tar, and no chemical additives, making it a relatively safe activity on the vice scale. As America and many other parts of the world get hosed, manufacturers in the Mideast are very happy hookahs. Hookah Brothers, a Cairo-based company, is moving more than 4,000 pipes a month to clients in 47 American states, a big part of their 400% increase in sales versus a decade ago. Get ready for more Mideastern culture to transcend politics and become part of our atmosphere.

Don't bogart the opportunity to domesticize other staples of international culture.

FILM:
Bollywood

Hooray for Bollywood! The Indian film industry based in Bombay (now Mumbai) is booming, churning out 1,000 movies a year in 20 different languages. Bollywood films have long been the rage in Asia, Africa, and the Middle East, but are now making major inroads into the West's cinematic and cultural consciousness. Lavish, melodramatic, and with more song and dance numbers than a Busby Berkeley extravaganza, your typical Bollywood film is about three hours long and includes no sex (kinda like most first dates). With a population of a billion people and a growing number of NRIs (nonresident Indians), however, it's not surprising that the subcontinent's leading export is currying favor in the international entertainment market. Bollywood is already a $100 million business in the States, and films like *Lagaan*, recently nominated for an Academy Award, are making Hollywood mogels learn a few words of Hindi. 20th Century Fox is co-producing three Bollywood films with an Indian production company, which may be just the beginning of the biggest blending of East and West since La Choy chow mein. Go rent *Devdas*, the most expensive movie in Indian history, or visit Ebolly.com or PlanetBollywood.com to get instantly Bollyized. Bollywood is, of course, just one dimension of the larger trend steeped in the secular side of Indian culture. Besides mehndi, Indian inspired fashion, accessories, home décor, and beauty products are infusing the West's sense of style, bringing some much needed color and exoticism to our more minimalist, monochrome aesthetic. At runway shows like the Bollywood Fashion Awards, American designers such as Maura Moynihan (the daughter of the ex-U.S. Senator) and Diane von Furstenberg are sending models down runways wearing shawls, sandals, and bags that seem to have more gold than Fort Knox. From saris to backyard Hindu deities to Bollywoodesque cosmetics from M.A.C. like Aura nail polish and Smolder eye kohl, Indian pop culture is driving smack down the middle of the two-way street going through our global village. Bollywood is quickly learning the Western art of profitable product placement, with Cola-Cola partnering with the Indian film industry by using the movie *Kaante* to promote its soft drink Thumbs Up in India. Look for us to import more Asian culture to spice up our meat and potatoes menu as we export our recipes for marketing.

Go East, young marketer, to take advantage of our perpetual fascination with life on the opposite side of the world.

ANIMATION: Anime and Manga

What Japanese export is sweeping across America faster than a spicy tuna roll? Anime and manga, those fraternal twins of Japanese animation, are having as big an impact on global pop culture as Walt Disney did in the 1930s. Anime and manga had just an underground, cultish following as recently as a decade ago, but are now redefining both design and entertainment for an entire generation. Anime, a style (versus a genre) of animation used in movies and TV shows, borrows heavily from that country's deep pictorial and illustrative tradition. Unlike in the States, animation and film are considered the same medium in Japan, explaining why anime accounts for 60% of the country's movie business. As well, anime is for all audiences in Japan, often dramatic and emotionally powerful with complex, even philosophical narratives (rent the 1989 *Akira* or 2001 *Metropolis* DVDs to experience full anime impact). Much of what's produced for American television, however, blends off-the-charts cuteness with hyper action adventure, a nearly can't-miss formula for big ratings among kids and, increasingly, adults. The WB's *Pokemon* and *Cardcaptors*, Fox's *Digimon*, and the Cartoon Network's *Sailor Moon* and *Dragon Ball Z* are making kids cookoo for anime, with the latter also airing shows such as *Yuyu Hakusho* on its Adult Swim weekend late-night block. The real money, however, is in the merchandising, with *otakus* (fanboys and fangirls) stuffing Dragon Ball fruit snacks, action figures, and skateboards into their Dragon Ball backpacks. At anime filmfests and conventions, rabid teenage samurais get spirited away by role playing as their favorite characters. Like anime, manga—the Japanese equivalent of comics—is multi-dimensional and read by all age groups in much of Asia. 40% of all books and magazines published in Japan are manga, many of them of them huge bestsellers. Despite (or because) of its cultural quirks—odd body proportions and an even odder storytelling technique—manga is taking America's entertainment landscape by storm. Virgin Megastores carves out a whole section for manga, carrying and selling loads of *shojou* (girls' comics) and *shonen* (boys' comics), and studios from Dreamworks to Disney are scrambling to option more manga titles. American publishers of comics have caught the manga bug, with Marvel introducing a manga-esque line, DC turning *Batman* manganese, and Tokyopop offering dozens of "100% authentic" manga titles (read right to left and back to front) including the #1 seller in the States, *Cowboy Bebop*. As more Americans become familiar with the unique yet also somehow universal iconography and themes of Japanese animation, expect the lines between Eastern and Western entertainment to get increasingly blurry.

Pork out on Asian pop culture as we go daffy for non-Western forms of entertainment.

HOME:
Asian Design

East is also meeting West in our own backyards, quite literally. Asian home design, which has ridden a wave of popularity in this country every generation or so, appears to have moved in for good. More Americans are incorporating Asian furniture and accessories into otherwise very traditional Western rooms, putting some Oriental ying into our Occidental yang. Many are attracted to the inherent serenity and calming effect of Asian design as well as its timeless elegance, craftsmanship, and kid-proof durability. Because of its less chunky, more linear look and feel, many designers believe that Asian décor "completes" a house, serving as the glue that holds together a genuinely holistic aesthetic. Feeling it's time to take a little of the Archie out of your bunker? Put a box, chest, or basket from China, Japan, Indonesia, or Thailand or a piece of furniture handpainted by a Tibetan or Mongolian peasant next to that overstuffed recliner and *voila*!—your home's chi has been magically restored. Antique herb cabinets in cypress, camphor, and northern elm are being retrofitted as CD cases, and alter tables with lush patinas added to foyers and hallways to turn homes into shrines of good taste. Large Asian wardrobes are being converted into entertainment and computer centers and wine storage units, and pieces salvaged from colonial period houses and Old Buddhist temples like woodcarvings, wall panels, bronze bells, and Burmese silver swords used to accent grandma's Iowa farmhouse dresser. A greater Asian influence can be seen in the kitchen too through hidden appliances, trimless cabinetry, recessed lighting, and a more subdued color palette. By emphasizing the horizontal versus the vertical, using natural materials like wood, metal, and stone, and focusing more on texture versus color throughout the home, many leading designers believe one can create a tranquil environment that serves as an antidote to our stressful lives. But no truly meditative space would be complete without a 300-pound statue of a Hindu elephant-headed god. Courtney Cox, Donna Karan, and Elton John all have one made by a master Balinese carver in their backyards, bringing some good spiritual vibes into their personal gardens. Look for more of us to build elements of Asian design into our homes to create peaceable kingdoms.

Think of ways to bring global symmetry and synergy into your product category.

FITNESS:
Tai Chi & Qi Jong

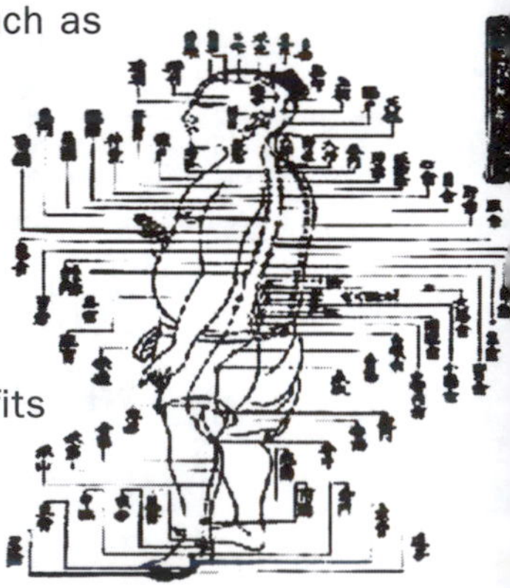

What's the most significant ancient Chinese secret since Calgon laundry detergent? Tai chi and qi jong, the slow, graceful exercise techniques that monks have done for centuries to greet the rising sun, are turning Westerner's heads. Based on animal movements, tai chi and qi jong are designed to improve the flow of chi or energy in one's body, the former done standing up and squatting with a constantly straight back and the latter done sitting or lying down. Tai chi classes at health clubs and community centers are filled to the brim as more Americans forego feeling the burn for a kinder, gentler workout. Most people who start exercising stop after a few months, the Oregon Research Institute found, but, because of its holistic, healing, and therapeutic approach, there are fewer dropouts with tai chi. In the classic "Yang" style, crouching tigers assume various "forms" or postures, such as "Grasping the Sparrow's Tail" or "Repulse the Monkey." The deliberate, slo-mo movements cross boxing and ballet, offering a paradoxically relaxing and meditative experience through intense mental focus. The health benefits of tai chi and qi jong, long known anecdotally by the Chinese, are many, now documented by Western medicine's best and brightest. Docs at Johns Hopkins found that tai chi reduces blood pressure, thereby easing hypertension and improving overall cardiac health—the same benefits of aerobic exercise but without the high impact strain. Emory University found that it reduces the joint swelling and tenderness associated with osteo- and rheumatoid arthritis and, by lowering one's center of gravity, increases leg strength and lessens the chance of falling (and not getting up). By improving balance, coordination, flexibility, stamina, and muscle tone, researchers conclude, older people can more easily walk, climb stairs, and carry groceries. Tai chi and qi jong thus have a domino effect impacting seniors' lifestyle as, when one feels better, one can be more active. Research has also shown that tai chi combined with guided imagery helped to lessen anxiety and depression among college students, making it much more than geezercize. The martial arts version, tai chi chuan, is also available for those who want a workout regime inspired by a John Woo film. Strike an Eastern pose as we find ways to lessen the stress that comes from working (and working out).

Shanghai consumers by allowing them to exercise their mind, body, and spirit.

TRAVEL:
Yoga Retreats

"Sometimes we must go outside in order to go inside."
—Slogan of Villas Pura Vida Yoga Retreat

How will you hear the knocking of true enlightenment when that boom-boom-boom bass from next door's spinning class is louder than that Who concert you went to in 1974? The number of yoga classes in health clubs has nearly doubled in the past five years, but those seeking both an inner and outer journey are heading to yoga retreats all around the world. Retreats offer yogis a real escape from their everyday routine, located in surroundings as peaceful, serene, and beautiful this planet has to offer. Even men, traditionally interested more in hard bodies than flexible ones, are doing headstands for yoga. At the Pura Vida ("Pure Life") Retreat and Yoga Center in Costa Rica, for example, one's day begins with a sunrise yoga session in a studio amidst the lush foliage of a tropical jungle. While toucans chirp away (sure beats the grunts from those sweaty muscle boys at the gym), one is guided through the asanas (poses) and pranayanas (breathing techniques) of hatha yoga, simultaneously cleansing one's chakras (energy points) and achieving "pranic healing" through the breathing exercises. Afternoons consist of immersing oneself in the natural environment by hiking along a volcanic crater lake, visiting a hummingbird and butterfly sanctuary, and river-rafting through the rainforest. Look out for monkeys, jaguars, and ocelots (oh my!). After one's chakra tune-up and eco-adventure, guests bunk down in luxurious "tentalows," a hybrid of a tent and a bungalow. Other heavy breathers are headed to yoga retreats set among the Inca ruins of Pisq and Machu Picchu in the Peruvian Andes and the Mayan ruins at Maya Tulum in Mexico, an isolated beach on the Yucatan peninsula along the turquoise Caribbean Sea. Power yoga guru Baron Baptiste occasionally drops in at Maya Tulum to teach classes in the large palapa (studio), making it a destination even for other yoga instructors. An outfit aptly called Inward Bound leads groups in anusara, a unique style of yoga at Locando del Gallo in the Umbria countryside of Italy. After three hours of anusara ("flowing with grace") in the morning and an afternoon of restorative yoga, guests take in the local eco-tourism which here consists of visits to local weavers, wool dyers, and, conveniently, the local Prada outlet. If none of these sounds appealing enough, hatha and ashtanga vinyasa yoga await on Clare Island near Dublin, Ireland, a place reported to have high levels of clear energy. Expect more of us to bend over backwards to realign our physical and spiritual selves along the journey of life.

Make inner peace the mantra of your brand.

SPIRITUALITY:
American Buddhism

"To do no evil; To cultivate good; To purify one's mind: This is the teaching of the Buddhas."—The Dhamnapada

Got Zen? Growing numbers of Americans are being drawn to the various branches of Buddhism (Zen, Tibetan, Pure Land, Vipassana, Theravaden), attracted to the religion's simple yet profound message to live in the present and focus on the now. In our complex, chaotic, 24/7 world, it's not surprising that Buddhism's principles of thinking about one's place in the world and committing not to harm others is finding special resonance. Many are finding Buddhism's emphasis on enlightenment an attractive alternative to Judeo-Christian religions which, let's face it, can be a tad judgmental and a smidge obsessed with sin. When you don't have to worry about how the world started or what will happen when one dies, some Western converts believe, it allows you to focus on what one ought to do today. Some Christians and Jews are integrating Buddhist concepts into their own religions and applying them in their daily lives. This more modern, secularized version of Buddhism, often called "American Buddhism," can be used as the basis for social and political action, to engage in things that will be of benefit to others. Buddhism has also become big business, appealing to our desire to surround ourselves with good dharma. Gaus (ornamental charms), meditation carpets, altars (bowl, statue, and lamp included), and incense are flying off the shelves like Nepalese hotcakes, considered sacred and beautiful icons of Buddhism. As well, a cottage industry of publishers and bookstores specializing in Buddhism has sprung up, and a number of organizations like the Institute of Zen Studies and the Stanford Center for Buddhist Studies are offering educational programs in the religion. The more adventurous are going further to see Buddhism in historical context, heading off the beaten path to follow in the literal footsteps of Buddha in search of wisdom and enlightenment. 21st century pilgrims are bound for Nepal and India, tracking his quest there for Nirvana (little did he know he could have found them in Seattle in the early 1990s). With a philosophy of tolerance, non-violence, and love for all creatures great and small, it's not surprising that Buddhism is closing the gap between East and West. The lesson to be learned here, little grasshopper? The best things in life really are free.

Present your brands as temples of peace and love among family and friends.

VOLUNTEERING: Peace Corps

"Upgrade your memories, download the world."
—Peace Corps advertising headline

After 30 years of declining interest and involvement in civic life, more Americans are again asking not what their country can do for them, but rather what they can do for their country. Since then presidential candidate JFK called upon Americans to spread goodwill around the world in 1960 though we would become the Peace Corps, more than 165,000 citizens have traveled to 135 countries as volunteers. But now record numbers are lining up to join up as the downward turn of the economy, dot-com implosion, and President Bush's State of the Union call for more volunteers drive the peace train. And since 9/11, applications to the Peace Corps are up 20%, reflecting Americans' greater awareness as members of the global community. Applications to other volunteer organizations such as AmeriCorps and Teach for America have nearly doubled and tripled respectively, confirming that something is definitely circulating in the altruistic air. 7,000 Peace Corps volunteers are currently working in 70 countries, many of them ex-dot-commers now developing an entirely different kind of content and expressing their desire to network with the real world. With many 20-somethings' careers on hiatus (the average age of a Peace Corps volunteer is 28), applicants are wisely concluding that a two year stint working in a foreign country will be a much more meaningful and rewarding experience than having to repeatedly ask that dreaded question, "Any coupons today?" After completing a 12-page application, surviving a lengthy interview process, and passing all the health examinations, peaceniks are "nominated" to a particular country. In exchange for a living wage," 24 vacation days, and about $6,000 upon completion of their assignment, volunteers do field work in education, business, the environment, agriculture, health, and community service. Volunteers go through a 3-month training period upon arrival in a foreign country, learning the language and local customs before they are turned loose as American ambassadors. Peace Corps alumni typically report that their gig is an unforgettable experience, truly "the toughest job you'll ever love," as the Corps' slogan goes. With the ambitious growth plans proposed for the Peace Corps which would double the number of volunteers and award a higher completion stipend, look for more Americans to go abroad in the name of service, dedication, and idealism.

Capitalize on our desire to feel and act like a citizen of the world.

TREND COMMANDMENT 9
Think (and Act) Global.

KA-CHING!

Use Asian design principles—hidden electronics, horizontal lines, stone materials—to allow consumers to drive in an Easterly direction.

BEAUTY

Mine beauty customs from other countries and incorporate them in your brands.

ENTERTAINMENT & MEDIA

Scour the global entertainment and media landscape for genres, styles, and properties that should be enjoyed by a wider audience.

FASHION

Develop a line of world clothing that melds European, Asian, and African elements.

FINANCE

Create a mutual fund of companies which are thinking (and acting) globally.

FOOD & BEVERAGE

Hold a mixed marriage for your next product by wedding ingredient X from the East with ingredient Y from the West.

HEALTHCARE

Promote a best-of-both-worlds philosophy in your marketing communications by endorsing complementary medicine.

RETAIL

Spice up the generic blandness of many retail environments by bringing some international flavors to your store's design and product mix.

TECHNOLOGY

Look East for innovation when it comes to all things technology. Who else but the Japanese would think up a robot dog?

TRAVEL & HOSPITALITY

Model your company after Luaka Bop by blazing the tourism trail to the four corners of the Earth.

TREND COMMANDMENT 10

Mine the Past.

TREND COMMANDMENT 10
Mine the Past.

"WASHINGTON- At a press conference Monday, U.S. Retro Secretary Anson Williams issued a strongly worded warning of an imminent 'national retro crisis,' cautioning that 'if current levels of U.S. retro consumption are allowed to continue unchecked, we may run entirely out of past by as soon as 2005."
—The Onion

Future schmuture. Although predictions and forecasts make good headlines, the reality is that America is more obsessed with the past than the future. This country is, at the beginning of the 21st century, steeped in the past, perhaps more so than any other society in history. The faster we hurtle into the future, in fact, the more we seem to use the past as a cultural anchor to slow down the pace of our 24/7 world and as a common denominator that our diverse, fragmented society can share. The past acts as a vital agent of stability in our time of sweeping digitalization, everyday biological revolutions, and major demographic upheaval, offering us a sense of familiarity and comfort at the dawn of a new millennium. We're preserving and honoring the legacies of the past, reviving lost traditions and experiences, and looking in our cultural rear view mirror for the romance and glamour that has largely evaporated in our post-PC (politically correct *and* personal computer) era. The aging of baby boomers too is a prime factor for our becoming a Retro Nation, with millions of midlifers mining the past to relive their real or imagined youth (and get it right this time around). I call this fetishizing of history "retronation," a large-scale social movement encompassing many trends that serve as buffering agents of the uncertain future.

With the past not dead but a living, breathing organism, marketers can and should use "retronation," as an active resource by which to create opportunities out of memories. History is a post-modern grab bag from which virtually anything and everything can be retrieved and reconfigured, a giant strand of our cultural DNA stored in our collective attic. Here are some ways that the stuff of yesterday is being turned into tomorrow's nest eggs as you put on your mining hat.

ARCHITECTURE:
Historic Preservation

Mining the past sometimes means saving it. As historically or aesthetically significant buildings, neighborhoods, and entire cities crumble or face the wrecking ball, a growing army of citizens and organizations are working hard to preserve them. With not-so-fond memories of the devastation of much of our architectural heritage during the postwar urban renewal movement, we're wisely assigning a higher value on the physical landscape of the past and making concerted efforts to ensure its survival. The National Trust of Historic Preservation is the Great Dane of watchdogs, issuing an annual list of America's most endangered historic places such the 1963 Guthrie Theater in Minneapolis, the 1958 Gold Dome Bank in Oklahoma City, and historic bridges in Indiana. The NTHP also warns that there are 100 neighborhoods in 20 states where older houses face dreaded "teardown," a rallying call against the gradual McMansioning of the USA. In Ft. Lauderdale, for example, 2-story, they-don't-make-'em-like-that-anymore Mediterraneans are being replaced by "starter castles" that make Tara look like a bungalow. As these Luxembourg-sized, suburban-style houses move into older neighborhoods, much of the distinctive character of urban life is being lost, stirring many residents to block development wherever possible. *This Old House* magazine has joined the fray, asking readers to let them know of significant homes facing "reno or demo" deadlines.

Preservation boards and leagues and city councils from Chattanooga to Spokane are also squashing bulldozers like a bug. The Chicago City Council, for example, recently awarded landmark status to a historic stretch along Michigan Avenue and protected the building in which Woolworth's sold notions and potions for about a century on State Street, that great street. Knowing first-hand the value of preserving the architectural past, Miami has now turned its pink-and-green attention to saving its outstanding collection of 1950s modernist structures. The Miami Beach Historic Preservation Board has met little resistance in its effort to make sure that atomic chic buildings like the Radisson Deauville and Casablanca hotels are around for a future generation of tourists to gawk at. On an even grander scale, visionaries are renovating and blocking demolition of buildings in cities with unique, defining architectural styles, such as Palm Springs and Havana. Havana, in fact, is spending millions of dollars a year to keep its incredible art nouveau, art deco, and modernist design mamboing and cha-cha-cha-ing. More curvy than Marilyn Monroe, Havana's 1951 Tropicana nightclub was recently made a national landmark, a sign that the Cuban government recognizes the beauty and value of its frozen-in-time architectural treasures. Expect historic preservation to reach historic highs in popularity and passion.

Honor the past by doing what you can to perserve it.

HEALTH & BEAUTY:
Public Baths

Take a powder, Canyon Ranch. More men are foregoing the milk paraffin cocoon wraps and hot stones for an old-fashioned public bath, jumping into the steamy fray with full, naked abandon. Public baths—around in some form since ancient times—fell on hard times after World War II, a victim of suburbanization and changing mores about being in a room full of nude, sweaty guys. But, thankfully, the public bath is back, giving a new generation of men more interested in schvitz than glitz the opportunity to let it all hang out. Regulars at the Division Street Bath House in the Windy City, for example, swear by the bath's benefits of total relaxation, a peaceful environment, escape from stress, and even a sense of spiritual communion. Like its clammy Midwestern cousin, the Russian & Turkish Baths in New York's East Village offers the chance for the stressed-out to chill out. Since 1892, the Russian & Turkish Baths has been a place for New Yorkers to "experience an unexpected paradise," the baths claim, offering a "new old-world pleasure of being totally relaxed and spanking clean." Your balls-out, aero-aquatic journey begins in the Swedish Steam Room, a cherry wood sauna with an electric heater, and progresses to the Turkish Steam Room, a white-tiled box heated by radiators.

Sit or lie down on the wooden benches, and let the eucalyptus or lavender lull you into a state of bliss. Resist entering paradise, however, as now it's time for the Ice Cold Pool. Jump or ease your way into the frigid water, giving every nerve in your body reasonable cause to tell your brain it exists. Just when you're getting used to it, move on to the Russian Sauna, a room heated by an oven filled with 20,000 lbs. of rock that are cooked overnight. When you begin to resemble a campfired smore, pour one of the buckets filled with ice water over your head and you are instantly returned to reality. Finish off your excursion as a climactic yo-yo in the Swedish Shower, where three columns of cold water jets blast your body temperature to somewhere approximating normal and leave you squeaky clean. Drink the largest bottle of seltzer in existence and return to the outside world, a little dazed but all the better for it. The renaissance of the public baths provides a rare Old World experience for 21st century explorers, an opportunity to participate in a ritual embedded in our genetic memory.

Turn time-honored traditions into brand spanking new opportunities.

HOME:
Log Cabins

"Timber!," more Americans are declaring, drawn to the warmth, comfort, and rustic feel of log homes. There are more log homes than ever in the history of the world, in fact, 500,000 of which are in the United States. 30,000 new log homes are being built in the USA this year, according to *Log Home Living*, a big jump over the 7,000 that were sold in the mid-1980s. Log home construction is now a $3 billion a year business, says the National Association of Home Builders, accounting for a solid-as-an-oak 6.5% of the custom-built housing market. What's driving us (including heavy rollers like Arnold Schwartzeneggar, Tom Cruise, and Ted Turner) to get literally down-to-earth with homes made of sticks and mortar? Even if they are more likely to have marble showers and home theaters than stuffed moose heads and bearskin rugs, log cabins are retreats and refuges from the splintering of modern life. Log homes are about 15% more expensive than regular houses on a square foot basis, but prices vary widely depending on whether 21st century Honest Abes use milled logs from kits or hand-crafted logs shaped by artisans. Logs often come from Canadian standing dead timber, making one feel a little better to know that live trees were perhaps not turned into your entertainment room. Entire developments of woodies, such as the Colony, a ski resort in Park City, Utah, are being built as more Walden wannabees bark up the log cabin tree. Even the timber-framing method of construction, which began to fall with the advent of the sawmill in the mid-19th century, is experiencing a comeback among log home purists. And those who hear the call of the woods but feel a log home may be a bit too Daniel Boonesque are building tree houses for grownups in their backyards or accenting their houses with paneling or staircases made from salvaged wood. Weathered planks and period boards and beams from old factories and warehouses add character and charm to a home and put to good use "free-range" timber from deep forests cut down centuries ago. Grab your coonskin hat as we forage through the past seeking romance and soul.

Branch out into new frontiers by logging on to products and services well-seasoned by time.

TRANSPORTATION: RVs

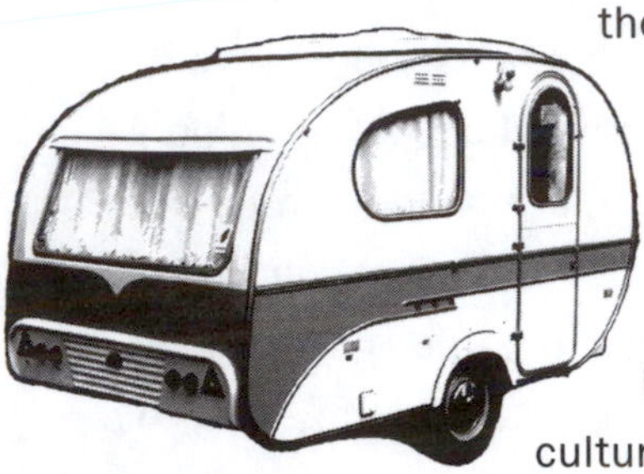

Where's Dinah Shore when we need her? More of us are seeing the U.S.A. through a windshield, taking the Great American Road Trip for the adventure and freedom it has offered for generations. Rather than Chevrolets or the ubiquitous postwar station wagon, however, we're piling into recreational vehicles, those hotels on wheels that make SUVs seem like Yugos. RVs started to climb up the cultural hill in the late 1990s but went into overdrive after 9/11 when going to the airport hopped over going to the dentist as our least favorite reason to leave the house. According to various trade groups, RV sales are up 20% in the past year, rentals are up 34%, and reservations for space at the nation's 16,000+ RV campgrounds up around 15%. Winnebago, the market leader with a 19% share of the $9 billion industry, is building a new plant to keep up with demand resulting from the best year for RVs in decades. Retirees are accounting for a declining portion of the 7 million RVs rollin', rollin', rollin' as baby boomers, the fastest growing market segment, get hitched. Like their parents in the 1950s, boomers are increasingly taking their family vacations on the road, an opportunity to spend some quality time together and become reacquainted with the nation's natural beauty and grandeur. The National Parks are not surprisingly a popular destination, with kings of the road often headed to Yosemite, Yellowstone, and the Grand Canyon to take in America's third most popular sporting activity, camping. Camping in an RV ain't like camping in a tent outside your father's Oldsmobile, however, with many of these babies packing queen-sized beds, satellite dishes, home theaters, heated seats, and washer-dryers. Owners love being in the driver's seat when it comes to traveling, not at the mercy of the sometimes less-than-hospitable hospitality trade. Besides being able to come and go as one likes, make one's own food, and sleep in one's own bed, snacks, a bathroom, and a nap (or time-out) are just steps away for the wee ones. Tailgaitaholics are also getting their kicks on Route 66, headed to the next Big Game or NASCAR race in RVs, and even business travelers are jumping into 'em for some serious (and fun) team building. With RVs offering control, convenience, and the thrill of not knowing what's around the next bend in the road, look for more of us to be captains of our own prairie schooners.

Put a tiger in your tank by fueling our desire for adventure and freedom.

COOKING:
Slow Food

*"Live Slow!"—**Slow Food Movement slogan***

It all started with the golden arching of the 18th century Spanish Steps in Rome in 1986. In reaction to the fast fooding of the world and our lives, Carlo Petrini founded the Slow Food movement, an international organization dedicated to make the kitchen table once again a center of pleasure and community and to living a slower, more harmonious rhythm of life. Petrini decided that it was about time, quite literally, that we stop and smell the tomatoes and declare war on the industrialization of food, the standardization of taste, and the homogenization of the supermarket. Through conscious (versus conspicuous) consumption and by prioritizing quality over convenience, Petrini and his slow colleagues believe, we can regain "much of what makes us human." Today the Slow Food movement is cooking in 45 countries with a worldwide membership of over 70,000. 21st century Johnny Appleseeds meet in some 650 "conviva," local chapters that support and celebrate the pursuit of happiness to be found through wholesome food. With the snail as their symbol and name of their newsletter, Slow Foodies are on a mission to preserve disappearing culinary traditions, cultivate and reinvigorate a sense of community and place, and reaffirm the creativity, passion, and beauty inherent in food and life. Slow Food is especially committed to saving our food heritage and the diversity of the Earth's bounty as thousands of varieties of fruits and vegetables and breeds of animals are lost due to modern agriculture's worship of efficiency and productivity. The organization's Ark of Taste project is making sure endangered foods like Moroccan oranges, Mississippi Delta barbecue, Minnesota wild rice, Green Mountain potatoes, and Sun Crest peaches are around for future generations to enjoy, believing that biodiversity is an essential (and tasty!) part of our cultural identity. Slow Food USA, which consists of some 5,500 members in 70 conviva, suggests more of us serve dishes built by nature rather than industry such as heritage turkeys and wild boar, and rescue traditional recipes, harvesting methods, and production techniques from extinction. The non-profit is also putting heirloom varieties of produce, handcrafted wines and beers, and farmhouse cheese on the menu, honoring past and present stewards of the land. Through any number of slow-as-molasses cooking ideas—using seasonal and local foods, squeezing your own OJ (apparently it comes from oranges), making homemade soup or pasta from scratch, or asking grandma how to make hominy grits or marmalade or tamales—Slow Food believes we can once again be seated at a splendid table and savor the best that life has to offer. Huzzah!

Help consumers eat, drink, and be merry by serving up tradition and continuity.

KITCHEN: Vintage Appliances

Just as smart appliances (Trend Commandment #5) are heating up, vintage appliances with more beauty than brains are also cooking, a perfect example of how oppositional trends can not only happily exist but feed off each other. As digital technology seeps into every nook and cranny of our homes and lives, we are simultaneously longing for relics of the Machine Age for their simplicity, durability, and sheer heft. Pre-counter culture appliances are fast gaining a cult following according to *Time Out New York*, as consumers park industrial strength stoves, refrigerators, toasters, and mixers in their kitchens. Weighing almost as much as a Mini Cooper and with enough steel, chrome, and fins to rival a '57 Chevy, a vintage stove is a nearly indestructible anchor in our disposable, planned obsolescence times. Plug in a cast-iron GE, Westinghouse, or Welbilt hog with two-tone enamel and porcelain knobs into the nearest socket and you'll instantly feel the unmistakable hum of built-to-last American know-how. GE Monitor Top Fridges from the 1920s and 1930s are especially sought after by collectors who in turn sell them to folks wanting "period appliances" to match their home and antique furnishings. And with few high-tech features, older appliances require less service and are quieter than new ones and don't require more energy to run. For those who don't want to go to the trouble of restoring and refurbishing originals found at salvage houses, kitchen supply stores, or online at sites such as AntiqueAppliances.com or MonitorTop.com, repros from companies like Heartland and Elmira Stove Works offer old-timey brawn and looks with all-new guts. Vintage toasters too are popping up all over, from 2-door self-flippers from the flappers era to Bakelite babies from the 1940s. Go to ToasterCentral.com or, of course, eBay to find an original or to Crate & Barrel for a Toastmaster red steel-and-chrome repro. Not surprisingly, housewares that look remarkably like those featured in the Nixon-Khrushchev "Kitchen Debate" are complementing vintage appliances to create what could be called "Ricardo Chic." Oneida has introduced recreations of Russel Wright's mid-century American Modern and Casual tableware, Anchor Hocking is once again selling Jade-Ite Fire-King mixing bowls and baking dishes in fifties-style opaque green glass, and KitchenAid continues to offer new colors (lavender, pistachio, and tangerine in 2002!) of its classic mixer designed in the 1930s. Expect vintage appliances and retro housewares to keep percolating as we try to ground ourselves in the stability of the past.

Counter digital technology with products inspired by our proud analog past.

FOOD & BEVERAGE :
Classic Cocktails

After a decade or so of sipping drinks in colors and flavors never intended by nature, classic cocktail culture is happily returning to your local watering hole. Pastel concoctions with plenty of punch but little pedigree are gradually wearing out their welcome as more bartenders discover original recipes from when a drink was a drink. Books like *173 Pre-Prohibition Cocktails* are making the literal rounds, unearthed by "mixologists" who are dedicated to reviving our cocktail heritage and diversity. Originally titled *The Ideal Bartender* when it was first published in 1917, the book was the first cocktail guide written by an African American and included an introduction by one George Herbert Walker, the great-grandfather of someone who knew a little about drinking himself, President Bush. Long lost formulae for punches, shrubs, and fizzes—drinks wildly popular in the early 20th century before the feds put the kabosh on John Barleycorn in 1920—are once again being shaken, not stirred. Cocktails imported to the United States from Europe after the repeal of Prohibition in 1933 like the Sidecar are bringing back a little of the glamour of the Ritz and Harry's New York Bar, the two Parisian establishments which claim to have invented the drink in the 1920s. On the eve of World War II, Americans were still mixing it up with drinks such as cobblers, fixes, sangarees, smashes, and swizzles, all documented in another time capsule being pored (and poured) over, the *Old Mr. Boston Bartender's Guide* of 1941. Cocktails from another golden age of drinking, the 1950s and early 1960s, are also back with a naughty vengeance as we knock back Gibsons, Grasshoppers, Old Fashions, Manhattans, and Negronis the way that Frank, Dean, and Sammy did. Even The Green Fairy herself, absinthe, is making an encore appearance about 80 years after being kicked off the American stage. All the rage in *fin de siecle* France among upper class bohemians, especially artists and writers, absinthe with its high (70%!) alcohol content and hallucinogenic properties were responsible for hijinks which make the Rat Pack seem like the Mormon Tabernacle Choir. The original version of absinthe is booming in the United Kingdom, Russia, Germany, and Austria, where it is still legal, and a less "psychoactive" version is now making American drinkers do another chorus of the can-can. Watch more of the high life bubble up as we try to quench our thirst for the real thing.

Add two parts authenticity, one part romance, and a dash of nostalgia to create a potent marketing cocktail.

FASHION:
Retro Sneakers

Just do it again. Sports shoes from the days of *Love Boat* and *Fantasy Island* are trampling the latest high-tech models, a genuinely classic case study of how sifting through the past can expose some big old nuggets. With many new models sitting on the shelf and being marked down, all the major athletic shoe companies are going old skool, bringing back editions from the 1970s and 1980s to appeal to consumers' love of all things retro. It all started in 1995 when Nike began reissuing earlier versions of their Air Jordans. Soon teenagers were skipping out on classes to line up around shoe stores, making industry execs realize the full value of what was collecting dust in their corporate closets. Now Nike releases one or two retro Air Jordans every three months, and rounds out its product line with other blasts-from-the-past like the Air Force I and Cortez. Nike's Dunk Low Pro SBs, limited edition skateboard shoes which originally debuted in the 1980s, are a runaway success, selling out in the first few hours they hit stores (and then quickly auctioned off on eBay). Other companies too are going to town wearing hand-me-downs, digging out classic molds from their archives and sometimes tweaking them with new color trims. With

product design already completed and big marketing support not expected (or warranted), profit margins are huge compared to new models with bells, whistles, and an occasional computer chip thrown in to boot. With its vintage styles from the 1980s, Reebok's Classics division is bringing in $450 million in sales a year, slightly more than its performance division. The company's Legacy line is inspired by art deco and mid-century moderne, while its Classic Aztec II model is more popular now than when President Ford kept bumping his head into things. New Balance too has joined the retro fray, while Adidas is opening up a collection of stores in New York, Berlin, Tokyo, and London called Originals, selling only classic shoes, clothes, and accessories. Smaller shoe brands whose heydays were in the 1970s and 1980s—British Knights, Keds, Pony, and, of course, Puma—are again running faster, jumping higher, and Converse has returned from its canvas grave. Long a symbol of iconoclasm (proudly worn by rebels from James Dean to the Ramones to the Boss to Kurt Kobain), "Chucks" are again strutting about in decidedly low-tech style. Original classics are especially sought after, with websites like ClassicSportsShoes.com selling Sauconys, Diadoras, and Tretons many of us wore to Wing concerts and aerobics classes. Look for more demand for the limited supply of yesterday.

Go into your company's attic to find a new market for old stuff.

MUSIC: Bluegrass

"We're so high-tech that I believe there's a longing in the human spirit—whether you know it or not—to have something simple."—Dolly Parton

Oh, brother! Since the soundtrack to the Coen brothers' film, *Oh, Brother, Where Art Thou*, went multi-platinum and took home record of the year at the 2002 Grammy Awards, bluegrass appears to be entering another golden age. Bluegrass was first recorded in 1940 by Bill Monroe when he turned Jimmy Rodgers's "Mule Skinner Blues" into a hybrid of gospel and old-time mountain music or what's been called "hillbilly jazz." Bluegrass is kinfolk with centuries old English and Scotch-Irish ballads, an Appalachian trail of banjos, mandolins, fiddles, dobros, and acoustic guitars combined with lyrics that tell a simple (and often sadder than sad) story. Bluegrass's second wind began to blow in the latter 1990s, a backlash against achy-breaky, phony-as-chicken-fried-bologna country music and the beneficiary of (blue)grassroots community building on the Internet. Today more fans than ever are being baptized as distribution finally catches up with demand and as bluegrass strikes a chord with our lust for traditional Americana. Album sales, concert bookings, and festivals are up, more retail stores are creating bluegrass sections, and more country labels, such as MCA Nashville and Universal South, are signing bluegrass artists. New pickers such as Nickel Creek are streaming down the mountain while veterans like Dolly Parton remember their bluegrass roots and Nashville cats like Alison Krause, Ralph Stanley, and Del McCoury feast while the griddle is hot. There are bluegrass tribute albums to Eric Clapton, U2, and Led Zeppelin, and a band named Luther Wright and the Wrongs have set Pink Floyd's entire 1979 classic "The Wall" to bluegrass. *Billboard* magazine recently launched a separate bluegrass chart (spinning it off from got-too-big-for-its-own-boots country music) and more radio stations are going red, white, and bluegrass. Over 800 radio stations program bluegrass music an average of six hours per week, according to the International Bluegrass Music Association, more than double the number of stations in 1996. XM radio, the satellite station, has an all-blue bluegrass station, and the CMT network is playing more of the music after its "Bluegrass Rules" weekend brought in ratings that were hardly second fiddle. Corporate America is slowly jumping on the bluegrass bandwagon, with Pizza Hut sponsoring shows and various advertisers using the music in their commercials. As a genuine, comforting, and soulful art form, bluegrass resonates with our deep desire for craft and substance. Listen for other spiritual echoes from the past to heal us in the present.

Harmonize with the amazing grace that dwells within our cultural heritage.

BUSINESS:
Bartering

Wanna swap? That's what more adults are asking as they rediscover their inner child and a business model whose heyday was a few thousand years ago. Bartering has always been around but has more than doubled

over the past decade as individuals, mom and pops, and Fortune 500 companies trade goods and services with nary a penny exchanging hands. Bartering picked up steam in the 1990s when many dot.-coms used it to boost revenues as part of some accounting not-so-funny business. Bartering has surged in the recent recession, as sure a sign as any that the economy is in the crapper. (Bartering accounted for almost half of all business transactions in the former Soviet Union before the Russian economy crashed and burned in 1998 and is used by more than 2.5 million people from all segments of society in cash-poor Argentina.) Here in the States, the International Reciprocal Trade Association estimates that $8 billion of bartering takes place through hundreds of formal networks or exchanges with another $5 billion in horse trading occurring on an informal basis. 60% of New York Stock Exchange companies use bartering to liquidate surplus inventories and for other big-time wheelin' and dealin'. But it is the give-you-a-chicken-if-you-horseshoe-my-horse kind of bartering that is upsetting the cash-is-king apple cart. Personal trainers are trading out their expertise for public relations services, dentists swapping root canals for painting jobs, and radio stations offering free time for signage at local retailers. Traders find each other through business organizations, the good old Yellow Pages, and online at sites like WhosBartering.com. Vacationers are trading homes to stay in at HomeExchange.com, and computer and video games e-swapped on the Games Trading Zone (Gametz.com). One of the more interesting bartering programs is the hogs-for-tuition plan offered by Lindenwood University in St. Charles, Missouri. Students from family farms with more porkers than dollars pay for part of their tuition with hogs, which are promptly processed and served up as bacon, sausage, and ham in the university's cafeteria. Talk about vertical integration! Watch us pig out on bartering as more consumers rediscover the original way to acquire goods and services.

Get in on the bartering action by offering a discount to consumers who volunteer time to approved causes.

TREND COMMANDMENT 10
Mine the Past.

KA-CHING!

AUTOS
Rescue automobiles from the rust heap of history by offering neo-models from yesteryear.

BEAUTY
Study beauty paradigms of the past and turn them into future products and services.

ENTERTAINMENT & MEDIA
Recapture the echoes of yesterday's rich musical and cinematic legacy for an audience hungry for the real and the original.

FASHION
Combine styles from the past with today's high-tech fibers to make clothes even better than they used to.

FINANCE
Take the stress out of money management by simplifying your products, plans, and communications.

FOOD & BEVERAGE

Scour through old cookbooks and create new products and recipes first intended for the cast iron stove and the icebox.

HEALTHCARE

Counter the scary scenarios of biotechnology with old-fashioned cures that grandma used to use.

RETAIL

Escort your customers down memory lane by adding artifacts of your product category's past to store design.

TECHNOLOGY

Make your hardware more people-friendly by putting the technoguts into a retro shell.

TRAVEL & HOSPITALITY

Allow travelers to literally go back to the past by marketing trips to less well-known sites of historical significance.

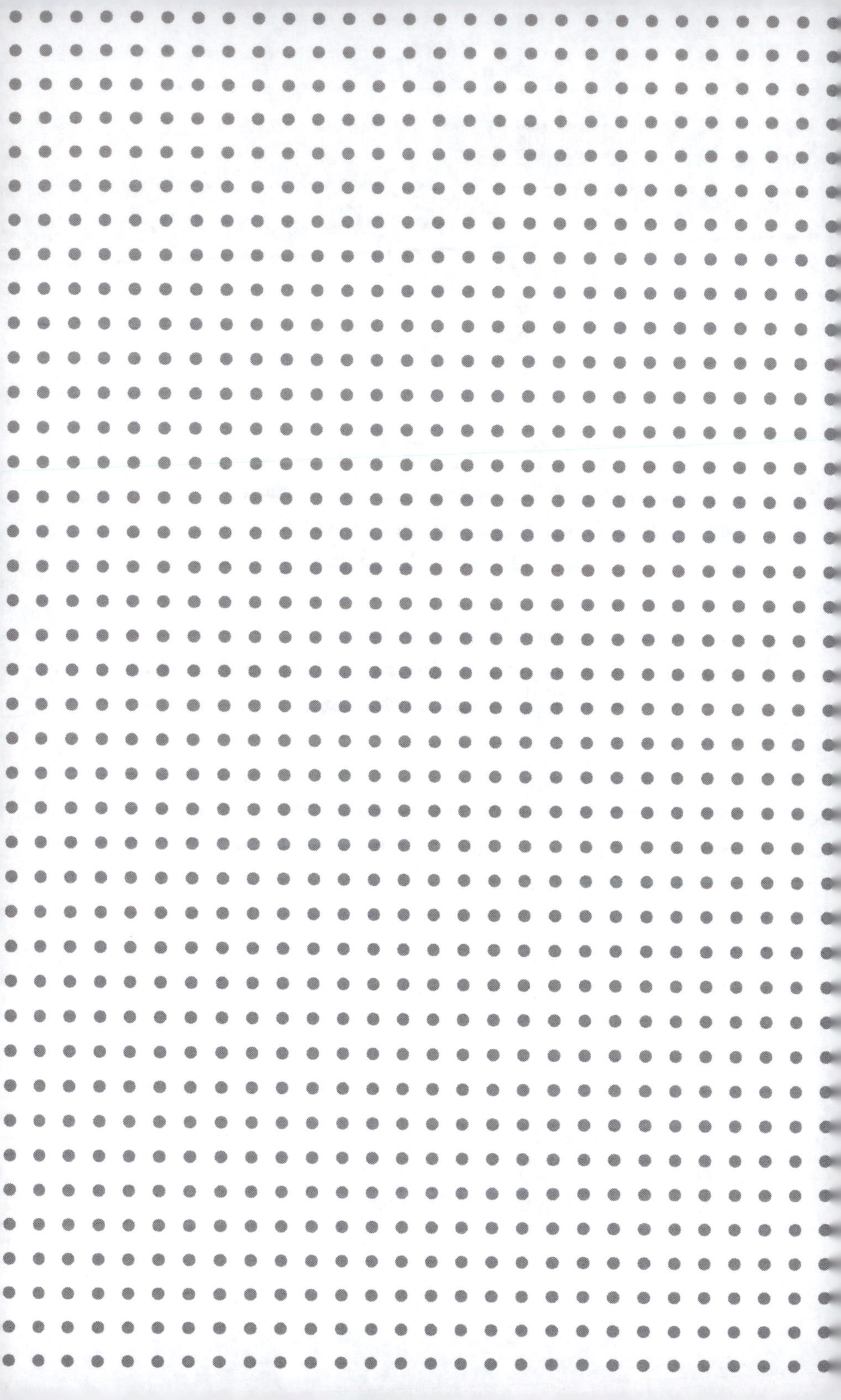

ENDNOTES

TREND COMMANDMENT 1: *Stir Passion.*

INVESTING : Socially Responsible Funds

Karen Krebsbach, "Socially Responsible Investing is Making the World a Richer Place," *Bank Investment Marketing*, November 2001, Vol. 9 Issue 11, p54; Thomas M. Parris, "Resources for Socially Responsible Investing," *Environment*, November 2001, Vol. 43 Issue 9, p3; Janet Kidd Stewart, "Socially Conscious Funds Losing Fewer Investors During Downturn," *Chicago Tribune*, November 12, 2001; Mike Kennedy, "Socially Screened Funds Hold Their Own," *Pensions & Investments*, November 12, 2001, Vol. 29 Issue 23, p24; Ali Velshi and Amy Petty (guest), "Socially Conscious Investing," *Business Unusual* (CNNfn), April 22, 2002; Susan Scherreik, "Following Your Conscience is Just a Few Clicks Away," *Business Week*, May 13, 2002, Issue 3782, p116; Amy Tsao, "Not So Bad at Do-Gooder Funds," *Business Week Online*, August 1, 2002; Tony Lystra, "Socially Responsible Funds Gain in Popularity," *Mutual Fund Market News*, August 5, 2002, Vol. 10 Issue 30, p1; Jo-Ann Johnston, "Analysts Seek to Explain Growth of Socially Responsible Mutual Funds," *Tampa Tribune*, August 19, 2002.

INHERITANCE : Ethical Wills

Michael Paulson, "Giving More Than Money: Ethical Wills Gain Favor," *The Boston Globe*, July 5, 2001; Bob Edwards, "Profile: Ethical Wills," *Morning Edition* (NPR), December 21, 2001; Jane Glenn Haas, "Ethical Wills Help Preserve Values," *The Orange County Register*, January 29, 2002; Kate Murphy, "The Virtues and Values of an Ethical Will," *Business Week*, April 8, 2002, Issue 3777, p83; Pat Arnow, "Leave a Message," *Reader's Digest*, June 2002, Vol. 160 Issue 962, p198.

SPORTS : Fantasy Leagues

Matthew Purdy, "Who's on First? Wonder No More," *The New York Times*, June 7, 2001, pG1; Michael Hiestand, "NASCAR Making a Run at Fantasy Game Circuit," *USA Today*, February 15, 2002; Rick Reilly, "Rotisserie Roast," *Sports Illustrated*, April 22, 2002, Vol. 96 Issue 17, p92.

WORK : Office Romances

Risa Brim, "Office Romances Get Mixed Reviews Among Kentucky Workers," *Lexington Herald-Leader*, February 11, 2002; Ambi Biggs, "Many Firms Lack Policy on Office Romances," *Free Lance-Star* (Virginia), February 14, 2002; Roger Franklin, "Office Romances: Conduct Unbecoming?," *Business Week Online*, February 14, 2002; "Elle and MSNBC.com's 'Office Sex and Romance' Survey Asks 31,207 People What Really Goes on in Today's Workplace," *PR Newswire*, May 13, 2002; Ann Oldenburg, "Quiet on the Set: Celebrities Hooking Up," *USA Today*, September 6, 2002, p11d; Jerry Thomas, "The Do's and Don'ts of Office Romances," *Ebony*, October 2002, Vol. 57 Issue 12, p140.

RELATIONSHIPS : Same-Sex Marriages

Dan Allen, "Gay Marriage Worldwide," *Advocate*, January 22, 2002, Issue 854/855, p22; Reed Irvine, "Same-Sex Marriage on the March or on the Rocks?," *Human Events*, January 28, 2002, Vol. 58 Issue 4, p17; Stacy Downs, "Kansas Case Debates Transsexual Rights, Same-Sex Marriages," *The Kansas City Star*, March 6, 2002; "Same-Sex Support," *USA Today*, March 21, 2002; Jon Meacham, Julie Scelfo, David France, Anne Underwood, Erik Amfitheatrof, Robert Blair, Sally Kaiser, "II. Celibacy & Marriage," *Newsweek*, May 6, 2002, Vol. 139 Issue 18, p42; "Marriage Amendment Proposed in House," *Associated Press Online*, May 15, 2002; "Times Will Begin Reporting Gay Couples' Ceremonies," *The New York Times*, August 18, 2002, Vol. 151 Issue 52214, p30.

SECURITY : Spy Gear

Shira J. Boss, "Entrepreneur's Vision Yields Stateside Success," *Crain's New York Business*, September 24, 2001, Vol. 17 Issue 39, p28; Jonathan Takiff, "Photography is All in the Wrist," *Philadelphia Daily News*, December 31, 2001; Nick Pachetti, "Spy Games," *Money*, January 2002, Vol. 31 Issue 1, p22; Peter Krivel, "Stores Sell Personal Safety," *Toronto Star*, May 16, 2002.

TECHNOLOGY : Privacy Rights

Jacob H. Fries, "At Spy Stores, Era of 9/11, Not 007," *The New York Times*, February 20, 2002; Stephanie Armour, "Worker Background Checks Raise Privacy Concerns," *USA Today*, May 21, 2002, p1a; Robert S. Boyd, "Threat of Terrorism Breeds Host of Sci-fi Surveillance Technologies," *Knight-Ridder Washington Bureau*, May 24, 2002; Gary T. Marx, "At-Home Spying: Privacy Wanes as Technology Gains," *Los Angeles Times*, May 28, 2002; "70% of U.S. Consumers Worry About Online Privacy, but Few Take Protective Action, Reports Jupiter MediMetrix," *PR Newswire*, June 3, 2002; Helen Jung, "Fingerprint Scan Spurs Debate," *Los Angeles Times*, June 3, 2002; "Court OKs Random Drug Tests in Schools," *Associated Press Online*, June 27, 2002.

COLLECTING : Rare Books

Tom Belden, "Browsing Rare Books the 21st-Century Way in Philadelphia-Based Web Site," *The Philadelphia Inquirer*, June 18, 2001; Guy Lesser, "Browsing for Gold," *Harper's Magazine*, January 2002, Vol. 304 Issue 1820, p39; Sheryl James, "A Rarely Profitable Pursuit: Hunting Hard-to-Find Volumes is Fun for Bibliophiles, but it Won't Make You Wealthy," *Detroit Free Press*, April 3, 2002; Thomas K. Grose, "Treasure Hunt," *U.S. News & World Report*, May 13, 2002, Vol. 132 Issue 16, p47.

TRANSPORTATION : Custom Motorcycles

Jewel Gopwani, "American IronHorse Has Built a Niche for its Custom Motorcycles," *Fort Worth Star-Telegram*, August 31, 2001; Neal Karlen, "Roaring into Town and Saying, 'Excuse Me'," *The New York Times*, August 9, 2002, pF1; Robin Hartfiel, "Victory Says You Can Have it Your Way," *Dealernews*, August 2002, Vol. 38 Issue 8, p60.

TREND COMMANDMENT 2: *Spark Creativity.*

BEAUTY : Body Art

Claudia Kousoulas, "The Enchanting World of Mehndi Body Decor that Delights," *Mothering*, September/October 2001, Issue 108, p38; Rebecca Gardyn and David Whelan, "Ink Me, Stud," *American Demographics*, December 2001, Vol. 23 Issue 12, p9; Ronald Kotulak and Jon Van, "Pierced, Tattooed Skin is the Medium of Choice in College," *Chicago Tribune*, January 28, 2002; Linda Marsa, "What Body Art May Say," *Los Angeles Times*, June 10, 2002.

WRITING : Poetry Slams

Joanne Weintraub, "HBO's 'Def' Jams with Poetry Slams," *Milwaukee Journal Sentinel*, December 12, 2001.

EDUCATION : Music Lessons

Julie Lew, "Doing a Guitar Solo with the Web as the Teacher," *The New York Times*, May 3, 2001, Sec. G, p7; Linda C. Allardice, "Music Lessons Online," *Link-Up*, January/February 2002, Vol. 19 Issue 1, p17; Robin D. Schatz, "Your Inner Musician is Just Waiting to be Found," *Business Week*, May 13, 2002, Issue 3782, p120.

WORK : DJing & VJing

Christopher John Farley, "DJ Craze," *Time*, July 9, 2001, Vol. 158 Issue 1, p88; Carol Becker and Romi Crawford, "An Interview with Paul D. Miller a.k.a. DJ Spooky—That Subliminal Kid," *Art Journal*, Spring 2002, Vol. 61 Issue 1, p82; Gina Piccalo and Louise Roug, "City of Angles; A Director's Spin on Hip-Hop Deejays," *Los Angeles Times*, March 5, 2002; Mark Glaser, "Making Images Dance to a Rock Beat," *The New York Times*, September 19, 2002, pG1.

DANCE : Ballroom Dancing

Soo Kim, "Ballroom Dancing: The Stuff Dreams are Made of - but is it Sport?," *Toronto Star*, April 15, 2001; Eliza Wilmerding, "Ballroom Fever," *Yankee*, June 2001, Vol. 65 Issue 5, p87; Alex Mattingly, "Students at Owensboro, Ky., University Able to Take Ballroom Dancing Lessons," *Messenger-Inquirer*, February 10, 2002; "Ballroom Dancing—A Blend of Art and Sport," *Jakarta Post*, March 31, 2002; "Shall We Dance? Where to Get Put Through Your Paces," *Jakarta Post*, March 31, 2002; Nicholas Keung, "Take Me Out to the Ballroom," *Toronto Star*, April 22, 2002.

COOKING : Culinary Schools

Dina Berta, "Culinary School is In: Economy Boosts Enrollments to Record Levels," *Nation's Restaurant News*, March 25, 2002, Vol. 36 Issue 12, p20; Ameet Sachdev, "Chicago Culinary-School Applications Soar as Downsized Workers Seek New Career," *Chicago Tribune*, April 4, 2002; "NYTimes.com Launches New "Cooking with the Times" Online Videos with Jacques Pepin; Series of Twenty-Five Instructional Online Lessons Completed in Partnership with The French Culinary Institute," *Business Wire*, May 23, 2002.

HOBBIES : Woodworking
Katie Ford, "Various Projects Keep Woodworking Business Busy in Broomfield, Colo.," *Daily Camera*, May 28, 2001; Drew Fetherston, "Crafting the Future From a Vanishing Art," *Los Angeles Times*, October 7, 2001; Jerry Large, "Works of Our Hands Ease Burdens of Our Hearts," *The Seattle Times*, November 5, 2001; "Little Ones Big on Working with Wood," *Toronto Star*, February 23, 2002; Jamie Vinson, "Lexington, Ky., Man Enjoys Hobby of Woodworking," *Lexington Herald-Leader*, March 21, 2002; Nick Harder, "Tips on Working with Wood," *The Orange County Register*, March 28, 2002; Joanna Werch Takes, "Woodworking's Crumbling Gender Barrier," *Woodworker's Journal*, August 2002, Vol. 26 Issue 4, p46.

HOME : Landscape Design
Dick M. Cobb, "Designing Whole Landscapes," *Landscape Research*, October 2001, Vol. 26 Issue 3, p305; Bob Edwards, "Profile: Artist Topher Delaney's Broad Vision of the Role Gardens Can Play," *Morning Edition* (NPR), October 10, 2001; Denise Cowie, "Ornamental Grasses Add Texture, Movement to Gardens, Expert Says," *The Philadelphia Inquirer*, October 18, 2001; "Green Dreams," *Flower & Garden*, November 2001, Vol. 45 Issue 6, p26; Christopher Johnston, "Backyard Oasis," *Crain's Cleveland Business*, April 1, 2002, Vol. 23 Issue 13, p21; Anne Raver, "Unmown Florida: A Call for the Wild," *New York Times*, April 4, 2002, Vol. 151 Issue 52078, pF1; June Kurt, "Green Acres," *House Beautiful*, September 2002, Vol. 144 Issue 9, p112.

RETAIL : Handmade Crafts
Leslie Kaufman and Julian E. Barnes, "Homespun Activities and Purchases Have New Appeal," *The New York Times*, October 10, 2001, Sec. C, p1; Elizabeth Kelleher, "Arts-and-Crafts Stores Defy Retailing Slump," *The New York Times*, January 13, 2002, Sec. 3, p7; John Hopkins, "Chesapeake, Va., Store Features Items from Third World Countries," *The Virginian-Pilot*, May 29, 2002.

TREND COMMANDMENT 3: *Declare Independence.*

JOURNALISM : Blogs
Norah Vincent, "Antidote to the Liberal Monotone: Blogging," *Los Angeles Times*, April 4, 2002; Steven Levy, "Will the Blogs Kill Old Media?," *Newsweek*, May 20, 2002, Vol. 139 Issue 20, p52; "Blogging: Create a Web Soapbox," *PC World*, June 2002, Vol. 20 Issue 6, p53; "MSNBC.com Launches Weblogs; Online Journals Driven by MSNBC.com's Top Columnists," *Business Wire*, June 3, 2002; Daniel Roth, Evan Williams, Julie Schlosser, Noshua Watson, "A Blog's Life," *Fortune*, June 24, 2002, Vol. 145 Issue 13, p144; Matthew Schifrin, "Click Here to Refresh Thyself," *Forbes* (Summer 2002 Best of the Web), Vol. 169 Issue 14, p2; Craig Colgan, "Creatures from the Web Lagoon: The Blogs," *National Journal*, August 3, 2002, Vol. 34 Issue 31, p2323; "Blogging in the Free World," *Toronto Star*, August 11, 2002, pD10; Steven Levy, Ana Figueroa, Arian Campo-Flores, Jennifer Lin, Marcia Hill Gossard, "Living in the Blog-Osphere," *Newsweek* (Atlantic Edition), August 26, 2002, Vol. 140 Issue 8, p46.

EDUCATION : Home and Charter Schools
Martha Woodall, "Online Charter Schools Stir Up Controversy," *The Philadelphia Inquirer*, October 30, 2001; Richard Rothstein, "Home-School Education Often Transcends Home," January 2, 2002, Sec. B, p11; Heather Voke, "Customizing Our Schools," *Educational Leadership*, April 2002, Vol. 59 Issue 7, p86, 1p; Timothy Egan, "Failures Raise Questions for Charter Schools," *The New York Times*, April 5, 2002, Sec. A, p15; Philip Terzian, "A Schoolroom of One's Own," *Providence Journal*, May 22, 2002; Jose Cardenas, "Los Angeles; Sowing Home-Grown Education," *Los Angeles Times*, June 25, 2002.

WORK : Soloist
Agustina Guerrero, "Chicago-Area Temp Firms Match Tech Jobs to Freelancers," *Chicago Tribune*, August 12, 2001; Linda C. Allardice, "Freelance Writers Can Bid Online for Work," *Link-Up*, March/April 2002, Vol. 19 Issue 2, p16; Melissa Milgrom, "Independent Curators: Have Art, Will Travel," *The New York Times*, April 24, 2002, Sec. G, p28.

FILM : Indie Film
Beth Pinsker, "Want to See First-Run Indie Films? Join the Club," *The New York Times*, August 26, 2002 pE1 (L).

MUSIC : Indie Labels
"Indies vs. Majors: Surviving in a Nu-Metal World," *Billboard*, December 1, 2001, Vol. 113 Issue 48, p23; Rhonda Baraka, "Growing Up Fast, Indies Shun Major-Label Parents, Do it Better Themselves," *Billboard*, December 8, 2001, Vol. 113 Issue 49, p36; Ben Wener, "Indie Labels are Providing a Haven for a New Crop of Bands," *The Orange County Register*, April 22, 2002; Chris Morris, "Rockin' Indies," *Billboard*, May 18, 2002, Vol. 114 Issue 20, p26.

FASHION : Alternative Jeans
Catherine Curan, "Decorated Denim Makes a Splash in the Jeans Pool," *Crain's New York Business*, July 9, 2001, Vol. 17 Issue 28, p4; Allison Fass, "Two Jeans Makers Want to Capitalize on the All-American Comfort and Fit of Denim Slacks," *The New York Times*, August 9, 2001, Sec. C, p5; Leslie Kaufman, "Levi Strauss to Close 6 U.S. Plants and Lay Off 3,300," *The New York Times*, April 9, 2002, Sec. C, p2; Dale Kasler, "Gap, Levi Strauss Flunk the Cool Factor as Young Shoppers Flee," *The Sacramento Bee*, April 27, 2002; Belinda Luscombe and Andrea Sachs, "Here Come the Fancy Pants," *Time*, June 3, 2002, Vol. 159 Issue 22, p72; Allison Samuels, "It's All in the Jeans," *Newsweek*, June 24, 2002, Vol. 139 Issue 25, p90; Olivia Barker, "Nothing Comes Between Teens and Their Jeans—Not Even...," *USA Today*, September 5, 2002, p1d; Susan Chandler, "Distressed Levi Finds Pockets of Success," *Chicago Tribune*, September 19, 2002.

SHOPPING : Indie Retail
Rah Bickley, "Durham, N.C., Neighborhood Enjoys Growth Spurt," *The News & Observer*, January 29, 2002; Stefanie Scott, "Retailers Target Younger Crowd in Appleton, Wis., Area," *The Post-Crescent*, January 31, 2002; Audra D.S. Burch, "Tree-lined Boulevard in Fort Lauderdale is a Stroller's Paradise," *The Miami Herald*, May 20, 2002; Richard Burnett, "Orlando, Fla., Urban Village

Beckons to Small, Hip Merchants," *The Orlando Sentinel*, June 17, 2002; Debbie Howell, "In-store Candy Boutique Trend Sweetens Pot Through Kid Appeal," *DSN Retailing Today*, June 24, 2002, Vol. 41 Issue 12, p28.

HOSPITALITY : Boutique Hotels
Edward Iwata, "Boutique Hotels Cite a Unique Ambience," *USA Today*, April 9, 2002, p6e; Andrea Bennett, "Boutique Hotels," *Money*, May 2002, Vol. 31 Issue 5, p129; Stanley Turkel, "When Does 'Cool' Become 'Hot'?," *Lodging Hospitality*, May 15, 2002, Vol. 58 Issue 7, p15; Kitty Bean Yancey, "D.C. Lures Bouquet of Boutique Hotels," *USA Today*, June 14, 2002, p7d; Bryant Rousseau, "Boutiques Entering Meetings Mainstream," *Meeting News*, June 17, 2002, Vol. 26 Issue 9, p1; Randy Diamond, "In Industry Slump, Boutique Hotels Try to be Cool," *The Record*, August 5, 2002.

TRANSPORTATION : Private Jets
Mark Sachs, "Tuned In; Celebrating Guys and Their Gadgets," *Los Angeles Times*, January 28, 2002; Ann Donahue, "Showbiz Blazes Trail in Sky," *Variety*, March 25, 2002, Vol. 386 Issue 6, p8; John Woolfolk, "Use of Private Jets Takes Off among Business Travelers," *San Jose Mercury News*, April 4, 2002; Madeleine Brand, "Joys of Time-Sharing a Private Jet," *Morning Edition* (NPR), May 7, 2002; Andy Pasztor, "For Sale: Used Jet, Low Miles, Nice Interior," *Wall Street Journal* (Eastern Edition), September 5, 2002, Vol. 240 Issue 47, pD1.

FOOD & BEVERAGES : Artisan Foods
William Rice, "A Cut Above: Handcrafted 'Boutique' Cheeses Gaining Favor," *Chicago Tribune*, December 17, 2001; Kristin Eddy, "Back to Bacon: A Breakfast Staple Renews its Image with New Artisan Brands," *Chicago Tribune*, May 20, 2002; Chris Reidy, "Panera Bread's Bakery-Cafes Sate Consumer Hunger, Whet Wall Street's Appetite," *The Boston Globe*, May 28, 2002; Melissa Clark, "Why This Cheese Stands Alone," *The New York Times*, October 2, 2002, pF3.

TREND COMMANDMENT 4: *Deliver Experience.*

EDUCATION : Internships
Glenn C. Altschuler, "A Tryout for the Real World," *The New York Times*, April 14, 2002, Sec. 4A, p20; Andrea Perera, "Paying Dues in Internships," *Los Angeles Times*, April 22, 2002; Beverly Beyette, "Not Just Gofers and Girls Friday," *Los Angeles Times*, May 20, 2002; Laura Vanderkam, "Leaders-To-Be Disdain Summer Jobs, Lose Empathy," *USA Today*, June 25, 2002, p23a; Stephanie Armour, "Record Number of Teens Just Say No to Summer Jobs," *USA Today*, June 25, 2002, p1b; Ruth La Ferla, "Attack of the Summer Interns," *The New York Times*, August 4, 2002, Sec. 9, p1; Dawn Fallik, "Washington Internships are Worth it, Students Say," *The Tribune*, August 16, 2002.

HEALTHCARE : Massage Therapy
Reed Abelson and Patricia Leigh Brown, "Alternative Medicine is Finding its Niche in Nation's Hospitals," *The New York Times*, April 13, 2002, Sec. C,

p1; Janet Piorko, "Getting a Preflight Massage," *The New York Times*, April 28, 2002, Sec. 5, p7; Belinda Luscombe, Melissa August, Leslie Berestein, Esther Chapman, Nadia Mustafa, Constance E. Richards, Sarah Sturmon Dale, "Massage Goes Mainstream," *Time*, July 29, 2002, Vol. 160 Issue 5, p48; Warren St. John, "For Worn-Out Shoppers, a Mall Massage," *The New York Times*, September 22, 2002, Vol. 152 Issue 52249, Sec. 9, p1.

SHOPPING : DIY Retail

Ryan Lee, "Jacksonville, Fla., Store Lets Customers Build Their Own Stuffed Animals," *The Florida Times-Union*, June 1, 2002.

SOCIALIZING : Theme Parties

Alix Strauss, "Slumber Number," *New York Post*, February 21, 2002; Dana Knight, "Business of Pampering Finds a Grateful Clientele in Indianapolis," *The Indianapolis Star*, June 4, 2002.

ENTERTAINMENT : Digital Gaming

Alex Pham, "Game Design: You, the Machine, the Water and the Weather," *Los Angeles Times*, November 22, 2001; Alex Pham, "Game Design: Updated Shooter Aims to Stay True to Classic," *Los Angeles Times*, January 31, 2002; Maggie Cutler, "Got Game, Will Travel," *Newsweek*, April 22, 2002, Vol. 139 Issue 16, p67; "Rockstar Games Ships Grand Theft Auto 3 for PC to Retail Stores; Biggest-Selling Game of 2001 Heads to PC Platform," *Business Wire*, May 20, 2002; Chris Farnsworth, "Newport Beach, Calif., Video-Game Studio Becomes a Fan Favorite," *The Orange County Register*, May 22, 2002; Thierry Nguyen, "Knights of the Old Republic," *Computer Gaming World*, June 2002, Issue 215, p46; N'Gai Croal, "From Volleyball to Monkey Ball," *Newsweek*, June 24, 2002, Vol. 139 Issue 25, p92; Matthew Fordahl, "Yahoo to Launch Videogame Service," *Associated Press Online*, September 22, 2002.

ONLINE : Webcasting

Vandana Sinha, "Age-Old Death Rites Take New Form in Online Obituaries, Funeral Webcasts," *The Virginian-Pilot*, January 7, 2002; D.C. Denison, "Webcasting Makes Comeback by Settling for Niche Markets," *The Boston Globe*, February 4, 2002; "Easter Egg Roll to be Webcast Live on White House Web Site," *FDCH Regulatory Intelligence Database*, March 29, 2002; Kelly Yamanouchi, "More Executives, Salespeople Driving, Using Webcasts, Survey Reports," *Chicago Tribune*, April 22, 2002; Steven J. Bell, "Discovering Cyber-Lectures," *School Library Journal* (Spring 2002 Net Connect), Vol. 48 Issue 5, p16; Leslie Brooks Suzukamo, "Internet's Free Lunch isn't Over, but the Portions are Getting Smaller," *Saint Paul Pioneer Press*, May 15, 2002; Scott Spanbauer, "Listen to a World of Radio Stations on the Internet," *PC World*, August 2002, Vol. 20 Issue 8, p138.

TRAVEL : Adventure Travel

"Alaska Briefs," *Travel Weekly*, December 13, 2001, Vol. 60 Issue 99, p15; Rich Haddaway, "A Howling Good Time," *Boys' Life*, January 2002, Vol. 92 Issue 1, p16; Elizabeth Schleichert, "Mush, Mush!," *Ranger Rick*, January 2002, Vol. 36 Issue 1, p4; Toni Gardner, "Mushing," *Country Living*,

January 2002, Vol. 25 Issue 1, p34; Bonnie Miller Rubin, "Survey Reveals Signs of Travel-Industry Rebound," *Chicago Tribune*, February 23, 2002; Susan Stellin, "They're Strapping on the Backpacks," *The New York Times*, March 3, 2002, Sec. 5 p8; Laura Bly, "Adventure Travel Takes a Slight Detour," *USA Today*, March 8, 2002, p2d; Laura Bly, "Dare to be Adventuresome," *USA Today*, March 8, 2002, p1d; Yishane Lee and Gretchen Reynolds, "Where Next," *Sports Illustrated Women*, May/June 2002, Vol. 4 Issue 3, p127.

TRAVEL : Heritage Tourism

Linda Duval, "Going Native: American Indians Turn Tour Guides," *The Gazette*, December 17, 2001; "News, Tips & Bargains; Free for the Asking: Black Heritage," *Los Angeles Times*, January 20, 2002; Mary Ann Jannazo, "Tourist Bureaus Will Show Visitors Our Eco-tainment," *Crain's Cleveland Business*, June 24, 2002, Vol. 23 Issue 25, p16; "Powwow Now," *National Geographic Traveler*, July/August 2002, Vol. 19 Issue 5, p31.

VACATIONS : Fantasy Camps

Avery Comarow, "Cooking Up Your Special Dream," *U.S. News & World Report*, March 26, 2001, Vol. 130 Issue 12, p58; Avery Comarow, "Fantasy Camps Offer a Sweet Swing at the Real Thing," *U.S. News & World Report*, March 26, 2001, Vol. 130 Issue 12, p56.

TREND COMMANDMENT 5: *Get Smart.*

THEORY : Multiple Intelligence

"Explore Your Smarts with Multiple IQs," *Career World*, November/December 2001, Vol. 30 Issue 3, p1; Thomas R. Hoerr, "More About Multiple Intelligences," *Early Childhood Today*, January/February 2002, Vol. 16 Issue 4, p43; "Jumpstart.com Now Offers Parents Free Analysis of Their Children's Preferred Learning Styles," *Business Wire*, July 15, 2002; Tess Kalinowski, "A New Twist on Learning," *Toronto Star*, July 15, 2002; Diane Lamarche-Bisson, "Learning Styles," *World & I*, September 2002, Vol. 17 Issue 9, p276.

EDUCATION : Specialty Camps

Mary Lord, "Hey Campers, How's Your Fiscal Fitness?," *U.S. News & World Report*, August 13, 2001, Vol. 131 Issue 6, p33; Jennifer Beauprez and Kris Hudson, "Denver-Area Summer Camp Aims to Reform Computer Hackers," *The Denver Post*, March 18, 2002; Kathy Boccella, "Specialty Camps Range from Rocket Building to Spy Camp," *The Philadelphia Inquirer*, June 11, 2002; Robert Lipsyte and Lois B. Morris, "How Do You Get to Camp? Practice, of Course," *The New York Times*, June 27, 2002, pE1; Amy Cortese, "This Summer Camp Grows Young Entrepreneurs," *The New York Times*, June 23, 2002, Sec. 3, p9.

ONLINE : E-Learning

"UMassOnline Enrollments Grow 58% and Revenue Grows 82% in Fiscal Year '02; Students Cite Convenience and Quality of Studying Online," *Business Wire*, June 10, 2002; "New Approach to E-Learning is Needed to Tap into $14 Billion Market, Says Booz Allen Report," *Business Wire*, June 13, 2002; Anuradha Raghunathan, "Study Shows Job Training Via

Computer Has Grown in Workplace," *The Dallas Morning News*, June 30, 2002; "Cornell University School of Hotel Administration Brings Professional Education Online with eCornell," *PR Newswire*, July 1, 2002; "Boston University Partners with Embanet Knowledge Group to Offer New Distance Learning Degree Program," *Business Wire*, July 9, 2002; "OPM to Unveil E-Learning Web Site; Site Aims to Support Professional Development of Federal Workforce," *US Newswire*, July 16, 2002; John S. McCright, "E-Learning Scales Up," *eWeek*, August 5, 2002, Vol. 19 Issue 31, p32; "US State Dept Offers 30,000 IT E-learning," *ITTraining*, September 2002, p7; David Lustig, "A Primer on E-Learning," *Customer Interface*, September/October 2002, p34.

FAMILY : Family History
Margo Harakas, "Ellis Island Web Site Adds More Features to Ease Genealogy Search," *Sun-Sentinel*, March 5, 2002; Mary Wiltenburg, "Genealogy Goes Beyond All Those 'Begats'," *Christian Science Monitor*, March 6, 2002, Vol. 94 Issue 70, p16; David Dishneau, "Bibles Chart County's Family Tree," *Los Angeles Times*, May 5, 2002; "Are There Soldiers or Military Leaders in Your Past? This Memorial Day, Re-Discover Patriotic Ancestors with Genealogy.com®," *PR Newswire*, May 15, 2002; David Mattison, "Counting Heads Around the World: The Genealogy of International Census Databases, Part I," *Searcher*, June 2002, Vol. 10 Issue 6, p36; "New Family Tree Maker Version 10 Ships This Fall!," *Business Wire*, July 11, 2002; David LaGesse and Holly J. Morris, "History Lessons," *U.S. News & World Report*, July 22, 2002, Vol. 133 Issue 3, p109; Sarah Kershaw, "Destination Queens, In Search of the Past," *The New York Times*, September 23, 2002, pB1; Bob Tedeschi, "Tapping the Family Tree in the Digital Era is Now as Easy as Typing a Surname into the Computer," *The New York Times*, September 23, 2002, pC8.

HOBBIES : Amateur Astronomy
Julie V. Iovine, "In Backyards, Starry Appeal," *The New York Times*, July 18, 2002, pF1; Jerry Burstein, "Beginner's Sky," *Astronomy*, October 2002, Vol. 30 Issue 10, p82.

RECREATION : Chess Clubs
Arricca Elin sanSone, "Chess Gets Cool," *Parents*, March 2002; Reid Cherner, "Maryland School Strong on Boards," *USA Today*, April 3, 2002, p3c; "U.S. College Chess Teams Turn to Recruits to Improve School Image," *AP Worldstream*, April 4, 2002; "South Texas Border Kids Take Up Chess," *Associated Press Online*, April 25, 2002; Maya Bell, "Inner-city School Takes 5th National Chess Title," *The Orlando Sentinel*, May 29, 2002.

TRANSPORTATION : Smart Cars
Nedra Pickler, "Automakers Developing 'Smart' Cars," *Associated Press Online*, March 15, 2002; Ed Taylor, "Motorola Researches Car of Future," *The* (Mesa Arizona) *Tribune*, April 9, 2002; Doug Bedell, "'Smart Car' Systems Face Rough Road," *The Dallas Morning News*, April 26, 2002.

FASHION : Smart Clothing
"'Smart' Garments Headed to Market," *American Drycleaner*, September 2001, Vol. 68 Issue 6, p10; Thomas K. Grose, "Clothes that Say it All,"

Time Atlantic, January 14, 2002, Vol. 159 Issue 2, p47; Cynthia Crossen, "Facing the Elements in Battery-Heated Jackets, Antibacterial Fabrics," *The Wall Street Journal*, March 1, 2002, B1; Theresa Howard, "'Smart' Clothes Raise Stain Shield," *USA Today*, March 11, 2002; Chris Taylor, "10 Technologies for You and the Planet," *Time*, August 26, 2002, pA52.

HOME : Smart Appliances

Mike Langberg, "The Next Big Thing? Home Media Servers," *Knight-Ridder/ Tribune News Service*, January 9, 2002, pK7731; "Digital Hubbub: Consumer Electronics," *The Economist* (US), January 12, 2002; Peter Brown and Alex Romanelli, "Want a Home Network: It's Already Installed," *Electronic News*, February 18, 2002, Vol. 48 Issue 8, p14.

TREND COMMANDMENT 6: *Nurture Nature.*

GARDENING : Organic Gardening

John Ydstie, "Profile: Benefits and Increasing Popularity of Organic Gardening," *All Things Considered* (NPR), May 31, 2002.

RETAIL : Farmer's Markets

Daryn Eller, "Farmer's Markets a Trip to Bountiful," *Vegetarian Times*, May 2002, Issue 297, p34.

FOOD & BEVERAGE : Raw Food

Mara Schwartz, "'Raw Food Chef' is No Oxymoron," *Los Angeles Times*, February 17, 2002; Cathy Thomas, "Good Eggs: With Pasteurization, Recipes that Call for Uncooked or Undercooked Eggs Can Come Out of Hiding," *The Orange County Register*, April 15, 2002; Jerry Shriver, "Healthful, Raw-Food Trend is Picking Up Steam," *USA Today*, April 26, 2002, p5d; Elizabeth Bernstein, "Some Like it Raw- Egg, that is," *The Wall Street Journal* (Eastern Edition), May 3, 2002, Vol. 239 Issue 87, pw10; Caroline Bates, "Rah Rah Raw," *Gourmet*, August 2002, Vol. 62 Issue 8, p46; Florence Fabricant, "You Hear About the Chef Who Doesn't Use a Stove?," *The New York Times*, August 7, 2002, pF1; "Raw Deal," *Vegetarian Times*, September 2002, Issue 301, p14; Peggy Orenstein, "Totally Uncooked," *New York Times Magazine*, September 1, 2002, Vol. 151 Issue 52228, p52; "Cooking Style: Cool," *Bon Appetit*, September 2002, Vol. 47 Issue 9, p30.

CAUSE : Eco-Activism

Andrew Goldstein, "Too Green for Their Own Good?," *Time*, August 26, 2002, pA58.

ARGRICULTURE : Hemp Movement

"Hemp-Flax Paper in More than 1,000 Staples Stores by Earth Day," *US Newswire*, April 15, 2002; "Goods," *Vegetarian Times*, June 2002 Issue 298, p16; Alan Pell Crawford, "High on Hemp," *Vegetarian Times*, August 2002, Issue 300, p61; "Motorcycle Powered by Hemp," *Natural Life*, September/October 2002, Issue 87, p19.

HOBBIES : Bird Watching

James Gorman, "The Benevolent Bird Hunters," *The New York Times*, March 15, 2002, Sec. E, p42; Robert Siegel, "Profile: Bird-watchers in Maine," *All Things Considered* (NPR), April 3, 2002; Charisse Jones, "Audubon Comes to the Inner City," *USA Today*, April 10, 2002, p3a; Mary Tannen, "Nobody Here but 289 Birds," *The New York Times*, April 21, 2002, Sec. 5, p8; E. Vernon Laux, "After a Pair of Rare Sightings, Birders Converge," *The New York Times*, April 25, 2002, Sec. A, p24; Liane Hansen, "Profile: Bird-watching Competition Along the Texas Coast," *All Things Considered* (NPR), May 8, 2002; Michael Crewdson and Margaret Mittlebach, "New York's Wildest Love Affairs," *The New York Times*, May 17, 2002, Sec. E, p29; E. Vernon Laux, "Sweet Satisfaction in the Songs of the Wild," *The New York Times*, May 21, 2002, Sec. F, p3; Tom Weiser, "Birding in Central Park," *Newsweek*, June 3, 2002, Vol. 139 Issue 22, p65; Molly Millett, "Bird Feeders, Birdhouses Flying High," *Saint Paul Pioneer Press*, June 20, 2002.

PETS : Holistic Pet Care

Arden Moore, "Best Natural Remedies for Dogs and Cats," *Prevention*, March 2002, Vol. 54 Issue 3, p172; Ellen Tien, "The Really Pampered Pet," *The New York Times*, May 12, 2002, Sec. 9, p3; Shawn Messonnier, "The Natural Health Bible for Dogs & Cats: A Holistic Journey on the Road to Healing," *Total Health*, May/June 2002, Vol. 24 Issue 2, p47; Adren Moore, "Help Your Pet Heal Himself," *Prevention*, June 2002, Vol. 54 Issue 6, p182.

HOUSEWORK : Natural Cleaners

Marianne Rohrlich, "Aromatherapy at the Dishpan," *The New York Times*, March 6, 2002, Sec. F, p1; Cindy Hoedel, "Aromatherapy Cleaners Make Housecleaning a More Agreeable Chore," *The Kansas City Star*, March 21, 2002; Julia Tolliver Maranan, "Clean and Decorate a Natural Home," *Natural Health*, May/June 2002, Vol. 32 Issue 4, p79.

ARCHITECTURE : Green Homes

Donna W. Rogers, "Virginia Housing Authority Sponsors Environmentally Friendly House for Habitat," *Richmond Times-Dispatch*, March 25, 2002; Joseph Ascenzi, "Two Rancho Cucamonga, Calif., Home Builders Register for 'Green' Program," *The Business Press*, April 22, 2002; Julia Tolliver Maranan, "Clean and Decorate a Natural Home," *Natural Health*, May/June 2002, Vol. 32 Issue 4, p79; "AstroPower to Power Urban Renewal Project in Cleveland; Environmentally Sustainable Community to Improve Quality of Life Through Solar Electric Power," *PR Newswire*, July 23, 2002; Richard Lacayo, "Buildings that Breathe," *Time*, August 26, 2002, pA36.

TRANSPORTATION : Green Cars

Donna J. Israel, "'Green' Cars Offer a Cheap Commute," *Toronto Star*, March 23, 2002, pWH23; "Hot-selling Honda Civic May Stir Interest in Hybrids," *AP Worldstream*, May 15, 2002; Honda Hybrid Melds Technology, Environment," *Toronto Star*, June 3, 2002; Lawrence Ulrich, "Honda Civic Hybrid Means Well, but at a Cost," *Detroit Free Press*, June 28, 2002; Melynda Dovel Wilcox, "It's Easy Being Green," *Kiplinger's Personal Finance*,

July 2002, Vol. 56 Issue 7, p24; "Honda Fuel Cell Vehicle First to Receive Certification; Honda FCX Slated for Commercial Use," *PR Newswire*, July 24, 2002; Anita Hamilton, "Mean Clean Machines," *Time*, August 26, 2002, pA46; Leonard M. Apcar, "Illuminating High-Voltage Commute," *The New York Times*, September 22, 2002, Sec. 12, p1; Danny Hakim, "Automakers Look Beyond Electric," *The New York Times*, September 22, 2002, Sec. 12, p1; Danny Hakim, "Smokestack Visionary," *The New York Times Magazine*, September 29, 2002, p100.

TREND COMMANDMENT 7: *Build Community.*

ARCHITECTURE : New Urbanism
Janet Ward, "Back to the Future," *American City & County*, March 2002, Vol. 117 Issue 3, p32; Joseph Contreras and David Villano, "The 'New Urbanism'", *Newsweek*, June 10, 2002, Vol. 139 Issue 23, p36; Cathy Kightlinger and William J. Booher, "Urban Planners Test New Trends in Indianapolis-Area Neighborhoods," *The Indianapolis Star*, July 9, 2002; Rich Laden, "Traditional Neighborhood Developments Popular in Colorado Cities," *The Gazette*, August 25, 2002.

SPORTS : Minor League Baseball
Bill Pennington, "Minor Leagues Hit the Mark," *New York Times*, July 28, 2002, Vol. 151 Issue 52193, Sec. 8, p1; David Casstevens, "Hot-dogging Promotions Jazz Up Minor-league Baseball," *Fort Worth Star-Telegram*, July 29, 2002; Jon Saraceno, "Strike-weary Find Haven in Minors," *USA Today*, July 31, 2002, p3c; Mark Starr, "Minor-league Baseball," *Newsweek*, August 5, 2002, Vol. 140 Issue 6, p60; Mitch Frank, Jackson Baker, and Matt Baron, "Minor Miracles," *Time*, August 12, 2002, Vol. 160 Issue 7, p54; Thalia Assuras and Lee Cowan, "Minor League Baseball Hitting it Big," *CBS Evening News* (Saturday Edition), August 24, 2002; Stryker McGuire, "First Person Global," *Newsweek* (Atlantic Edition), September 9, 2002, Vol. 140 Issue 9, p6.

ART : Public Art
Derrill Holly "Washington's Newest Party Animals," *Associated Press Online*, April 23, 2002; Tim Nudd, Trevor Jensen, and Ann M. Mack, "This One Goes to 11," *Adweek* (Western Edition), July 1, 2002, Vol. 52 Issue 27, p38; "Polar Bears are Loose in Royal Oak!," *PR Newswire*, July 12, 2002; Nery Ynclan, "Old Submarines' Fins Resurface as 'Peace' Art," *The Miami Herald*, August 26, 2002.

GARDENING : Community Gardens
Lee Tucker, "Get Down and Dirty," *Prevention*, July 2002, Vol. 54 Issue 7, p45; Anne Raver, "From Rubble, Ingenuity Sprouts," *The New York Times*, August 22, 2002, Vol. 151 Issue 52218, pF1; Karen Madsen, "Green Havens," *E Magazine: The Environmental Magazine*, September/October 2002, Vol. 13 Issue 5, p16.

FOOD & BEVERAGE : Community Shared Agriculture
Angela Watercutter "Local Farming Changes Food Markets," *Associated Press Online*, July 3, 2002.

RELATIONSHIPS : E-Mentoring

Nora McAniff, "Inside People," *People*, January 28, 2002, Vol. 57 Issue 3, p4; "AOL Time Warner Foundation, Mentor/National Mentoring Partnership Announce Launch of 'Mentors Online: the E-mentoring Tool Kit'," *Business Wire*, June 10, 2002; Angela Gunn, "Working, Class," *Time Out New York*, June 13-20, 2002, p158; "JPMorgan Chase First Corporate Sponsor of Mentoring.org," *Business Wire*, July 15, 2002.

TRAVEL : Volunteer Vacations

Erika L. Dilday, "Vacation with a Mission," *The New York Times*, July 1, 2001, Sec. 5, p8; "Jo Broyles Yohay, "Volunteering on Vacation," *The New York Times*, December 23, 2001, Sec. 5, p2; Allen Holder, "People Give & Get Back During Volunteer Vacations Around the World," *The Kansas City Star*, May 6, 2002; Anna Kuchment, Barbara Koh, and Dune Lawrence, "Lending a Helping Hand," *Newsweek*, July 22, 2002, Vol. 140 Issue 4, p66.

FAMILY : Family Reunions

Mary Wiltenburg, "Genealogy Goes Beyond All Those 'Begats'," *Christian Science Monitor*, March 6, 2002, Vol. 94 Issue 70, p16; Renee Vogel, "Side Trips: Travel Tips, Trends and Tools; It's All Relative; Sibling Revelry," *Los Angeles Times*, March 17, 2002; "How to Plan the Best Family Reunion," *Ebony*, April 2002, Vol. 57 Issue 6, p118; "Black Family Reunions," *Ebony*, May 2002, Vol. 57 Issue 7, p56; "Getting Ready for the 2002 Reunion Season," *Ebony*, June 2002, Vol. 57 Issue 8, p46; "Families Together: Reunions Bring a Family into Focus," *Working Mother*, June/July 2002, p62; Carol Biliczky, "In Post-Sept. 11 Summer, People Feel Need to Connect," *Akron Beacon Journal*, July 15, 2002; Liz Stevens, "Reunions are Key Activity in Extended African-American Families," *Fort Worth Star-Telegram*, July 23, 2002; Elizabeth Lund, "Family Reunions are More Popular Than Ever," *Christian Science Monitor*, August 21, 2002, Vol. 94 Issue 188, p11.

CRAFTS : Knitting Circles

Eva Marer, "Knitting: The New Yoga," *Health*, March 2002, Vol. 16 Issue 2, p76; Kristina Sauerwein, "Help from a Tightknit Group," *Los Angeles Times*, April 8, 2002; Lisa Gutierrez, "Knitting, More Popular Than Ever, Isn't Just for Grandma Anymore," *The Kansas City Star*, April 23, 2002; Barbara Gash, "Need to Relax? Try Your Hand at Knitting," *Detroit Free Press*, June 6, 2002; John Wolfson, "Knitting Away the Worries, Weaving New Friendships," *The Seattle Times*, August 26, 2002.

TREND COMMANDMENT 8: *Surf the Edge.*

SPORTS : Adventure Racing

Wendy Cole and Sean Gregory, "Urban Extreme," *Time*, September 16, 2002, Vol. 160 Issue 12, p18.

TRAVEL : Monastery Retreats

B.J. Lee, "That's the Spirit," *Newsweek* (Atlantic Editions), June 3, 2002, Vol. 139 Issue 22, p60; Sarah Andrews, "Monasteries in Spain Offer a Truly Quiet Escape for Tourists," *AP Worldstream*, June 12, 2002.

ARCHITECTURE : Vastu Shastra
Jessie Milligan, "Goodbye, Feng Shui; Hello, Vastu Shastra," *Fort Worth Star-Telegram*, May 23, 2002; Samar Chandra, "True Ecological Enlightenment Begins with Interior Design," *Toronto Star*, June 18, 2002, pA27 (letter).

FASHION : Urban Apparel
Chris Reidy, "Reebok Markets Brand with Hip-Hop Parties," *The Boston Globe*, March 29, 2002; Jeffrey McKinney, "Rags to Riches," *Black Enterprise*, September 2002, Vol. 33 Issue 2, p98.

PETS : Pet Resorts
Hannah Fiske, "Jefferson, Pa., Pet Spa Allows Furry Friends to Relax in Luxury," *Knight-Ridder/Tribune Business News*, August 6, 2001; Dave Melendi, "Sun Valley, Calif.-Area Pet Resorts Encounter Decline in Business," *Daily News* (Los Angeles), October 24, 2001; R.P. Joseph, "The Dude Ranch for Dogs is a Canine Vacation," *Sarasota Herald Tribune*, July 4, 2002 pH10; Jerry Berrios, "Pet Resorts Give Fido, Fluffy a Taste of Luxury," *Knight-Ridder/ Tribune News Service*, August 5, 2002, pK7124.

RELATIONSHIPS : Tribes
Abby Ellin, "Tribes," *The New York Times*, June 9, 2002, Sec. 14, p1.

MUSIC : Outsider Music
Dwight Garner, "Band of Outsiders," *The New York Times*, March 17, 2002, p11 (L).

RADIO : Alt-Radio
Greg Edwards, "Some Question FCC's Fast Tracking of Digital Radio," *Richmond Times-Dispatch*, March 21, 2002; Ian Landau, "Radio," *Time Out New York*, June 13-20, 2002, p156.

LITERATURE : Comic Books & Graphic Novels
Scott Simon, "Alternative Press Expo Where Cartoonists Talk About Tension Between Gaining a Wide Audience and Selling Out," *Weekend Edition Saturday* (NPR), March 2, 2002; Jacki Lyden, "Return of the Comic Book 'Love & Rockets'," *Weekend All Things Considered* (NPR), March 31, 2002; "Boldly Going Where No Comics Have Gone Before," *News Bytes News Network*, April 12, 2002; John LeLand, "Like 'Dilbert,' but Subversive and Online," *The New York Times*, April 21, 2002, Sec. 9, p1; "If Sartre Read Mad Magazine," *Toronto Star*, May 11, 2002; Phinjo Gombu, "Artists Pay Homage to Beguiling Comic Store," *Toronto Star*, May 17, 2002, pC12; Sara Nesbitt, "Comic Books Undergo Resurgence in Popularity Due to 'Spider-Man' Movie," *The Gazette*, May 19, 2002; Raoul V. Mowatt, "At a Comics Store, a Life Less Ordinary," *Chicago Tribune*, May 20, 2002; "Oldsmar, Fla., Entrepreneur Hopes to Revive Comic Book Industry," *Tampa Tribune*, May 26, 2002; Lynn Neary, "Analysis: Comic Book Industry Fighting for Legitimacy and Income," *All Things Considered* (NPR), July 19, 2002; Scott Bowles, "'Perdition' Broadens Way for Graphic Novels," *USA Today*, July 25, 2002, p8d; George Gene Gustines, "A Comic Book Gets Serious on Gay Issues," *The New York Times*, August 13, 2002, Vol. 151 Issue 52209, pE1.

SEX : Sex Workshops
Catherine Porter, "Sex Toys Get Wholesome," *Toronto Star*, February 8, 2002, pF5; Rafer Guzman, "A New Course for High-End Spas: Sex," *Wall Street Journal* (Eastern Edition), June 21, 2002, Vol. 239 Issue 121, pW8.

TREND COMMANDMENT 9: *Think (and Act) Global.*

MUSIC: World Beat
David Hutcheon, "Mixing Up the World's Beat," *Mother Jones*, July/Aug 2002, Vol. 27 Issue 4, p74.

FASHION: Soccer Jerseys
Cara Griffin, "International Appeal," *Sporting Goods Business*, March 2002, Vol. 35 Issue 3, p42; Ginia Bellafante, "Front Row: Soccer Winner," *The New York Times*, June 11, 2002, pB8 (L); Bruce Horovitz, "Fans Make USA Soccer Jerseys Hard to Find," *USA Today*, June 18, 2002.

SMOKING : Hookahs
C.L. Kieffer, "Social Smoking Regaining Popularity," *The* (University of California Riverside) *Highlander*, Vol. 51 Issue 0; "Happy Hookahs," *Economist*, May 5-11, 2001, Vol. 360 Issue 8220, p40; Evan Alan Wright, "Hookahs," *Rolling Stone*, August 30, 2001, Issue 876, p74; Sal Pizarro, "Flavored Tobaccos, Exotic Ambience Target the Under-21 Crowd," *Mercury News*, July 3, 2002.

FILM: Bollywood
Ruth La Ferla, "Kitsch with a Niche: Bollywood Chic Finds a Home," *The New York Times*, May 5, 2002, p1 (L); Deepti Hajela, "Second Bollywood Fashion Awards Honor Indian Design," *AP Worldstream*, June 29, 2002; Richard Corliss and Jyoti Thottam, "Going Bollywood," *Time*, July 22, 2002, Vol. 160 Issue 4, p51; Renee Montagne, "Profile: India's Film Industry," *Morning Edition* (NPR), August 7, 2002; Mark Lowry, "Hurray for Bollywood: Indian Cinema Has Influence in America," *Fort Worth Star-Telegram*, August 12, 2002; Ranjan Roy, "Bollywood Begins to Break into Western Screens," *AP Worldstream*, August 27, 2002; Gabriel Kahn, "India's Bollywood Gets Wise to Lucrative Product Placement," *Wall Street Journal* (Eastern Edition), September 4, 2002, Vol. 240 Issue 46, pB5B.

ANIMATION : Anime and Manga
J.D. Considine, "Making Anime a Little Safer for Americans," *The New York Times*, January 20, 2002, p33 (L); Dave Kehr, "Anime, Japanese Cinema's Second Golden Age," *The New York Times*, January 20, 2002, p1 (L); Geoff Pevere, "Anime Packs Big Wallop of Ideas," *Toronto Star*, February 1, 2002, pD3; Amanda Rogers, "The World of 'Dragonball Z' is Expanding," *Fort Worth Star-Telegram*, March 5, 2002; Hera Diani, "'Manga' Comics More Than Meets the Eye," *Jakarta Post*, March 10, 2002; "Disney Has Japan's Spirit," *Video Business*, April 15, 2002, Vol. 22 Issue 15, p6; Marc Bernardin, "Video & DVD: Anime," *Entertainment Weekly*, April 19, 2002, Issue 649, p52; Terry Lawson, "'Metropolis' Will Thrill Anime Fans," *Detroit Free Press*, April 23, 2002; "Akira, Metropolis: Intro to Anime 101," *Toronto Star*, May 3, 2002,

pC2; Douglas Wolk, "The Manga are Coming," *Publishers Weekly*, June 17, 2002, Vol. 249 Issue 24, p29; Jesse McKinley, "Anime Fans Gather, Loudly and Proudly Obsessed," *The New York Times*, September 3, 2002, Vol. 151 Issue 52230, pE1; Susan Wloszczyna, "Disney Hopes Japanese 'Toon Casts U.S. Spell," *USA Today*, September 18, 2002, p1d.

HOME : Asian Design
Joy Krause, "Simple, Crisp Asian Design Swings Back into Favor," *Milwaukee Journal Sentinel*, May 9, 2002; Frances Anderton, "A Hindu God in Limestone for Inspiration and Luck," *The New York Times*, July 18, 2002, pF3 (L).

FITNESS : Tai Chi & Qi Jong
Eric Nagourney, "Arthritis Patients Embrace the Tiger," *The New York Times*, November 13, 2001, pF7 (L); Michele Stanten and Selene Yeager, "Kinder, Gentler Workouts," *Prevention*, July 2002, Vol. 54 Issue 7, p74; "Tai Chi: An Exercise You Can Stick With," *Tufts University Health & Nutrition Letter*, July 2002, Vol. 20 Issue 5, p2; Hallie D. Winchell, "Behind Tai Chi," *American Fitness*, July/August 2002, Vol. 20 Issue 4, p24; Christine Gorman, "Why Tai Chi is the Perfect Exercise," *Time Atlantic*, August 19, 2002, Vol. 160 Issue 8, p57.

TRAVEL : Yoga Retreats
"Great Escapes," *Fitness*, April 2002; Matthew Solan, "Going to the Source," *Yoga Journal*, April 2002; "Wellness Spas," *Spa Finder*, Spring 2002; Debra A. Klein, "Inner Peace, Good Eats," *Newsweek* (Atlantic Edition), April 22, 2002, Vol. 139 Issue 16, p68; Donna Wilkinson, "Guys are Warming Up to Yoga and Pilates," *The New York Times*, September 23, 2002, Vol. 152 Issue 52250, p9.

VOLUNTEERING : Peace Corps
Julie Murdock, "Education: More Helping Hands," *Newsweek*, June 10, 2002, p9; Dena Bunis, "Bill Would Provide Funds to Expand Peace Corps," *Knight-Ridder/Tribune News Service (The Orange County Register)*, June 25, 2002, pK3426; "Seattle-Area Workers Consider Volunteering for Peace Corps," *Knight-Ridder/Tribune Business News*, June 30, 2002; Greg Jonsson and Aisha Sultan, "With College Degree but Bleak Economy, More Try for Peace Corps, Grad School," *Knight-Ridder/Tribune News Service (St. Louis Post-Dispatch)*, August 9, 2002, pK2516; Sumana Chatterjee, "Sept. 11 Attacks Spurred Older Americans to Volunteer, Poll Says," *Knight-Ridder Washington Bureau*, August 25, 2002; Jonathan D. Salant, "Charities Report Surge of Volunteers," *Associated Press Online*, September 12, 2002; Joelle Tessler, "Peace Corps Offers Haven for Dot-Com Refugees," *San Jose Mercury News*, September 16, 2002; With Jobs Scarce, Many Heed Peace Corps' Call," *The New York Times*, August 18, 2002, Vol. 151 Issue 52214, p18.

TREND COMMANDMENT 10: *Mine the Past.*

ARCHITECTURE : Historic Preservation
Nicole White, "Miami Beach, Fla., Historical Preservation Board to Protect 1950s Architecture," *The Miami Herald*, February 18, 2002; Gary Washburn, "Chicago City Council Grants Landmark Status to Stretch of Michigan Avenue,"

Chicago Tribune, February 28, 2002; Elena Cabral, "Residents of Older Fort Lauderdale, Fla., Homes Dislike New 'Starter Castles'," *The Miami Herald*, July 1, 2002; K.L., "National Trust Names 11 Most-Endangered Historic Places," *Architectural Record*, July 2002, Vol. 190 Issue 7, p38; Cathleen McGuigan, "Saving Havana," *Newsweek*, July 15, 2002, Vol. 140 Issue 3, p52; Ryan Robbins, "Save This Old House," *This Old House*, September 2002, Vol. 7 Issue 7, p164; Mike Pare, "Preservation Group Rescues Historical Chattanooga, Tenn., Commercial Building," *Chattanooga Times/Free Press*, September 10, 2002; Kandis Carper, "Spokane, Wash., Holds Renovator's Fair for Its 30,000 Vintage Home Owners," *The Spokesman-Review*, September 20, 2002; Nicole White, "Miami Area Debates Condition of Art Deco Structures," *The Miami Herald*, September 23, 2002.

HEALTH & BEAUTY: Public Baths

John W. Fountain, "Broad-Shoulder Brotherhood, Forged in Steam," *The New York Times*, February 21, 2001, Vol. 150 Issue 51671, pA10.

HOME: Log Cabins

Gaile Robinson, "Cozy Cabins Hold Nostalgic Appeal for Increasing Numbers of Baby Boomers," *Fort Worth Star-Telegram*, January 3, 2002; Olivia Barker, "Buying Winter Wonderland," *USA Today*, February 15, 2002, p9d; Marine Cole, "A Guide to Building Your Own Log Cabin, from Snug to Sumptuous," *The New York Times*, April 12, 2002, pF8 (L); Matt Richtel, "A Return to Nature, Mostly by Cutting It Down," *The New York Times*, April 12, 2002, pF1 (L); Charles Enloe, "Building, Old-Style," *American Forests*, Summer 2002, Vol. 108 Issue 2, p22; Joseph Smith, "Logging on to Comfort," *Crain's Detroit Business*, June 3, 2002, Vol. 18 Issue 22, p21; Heather Won Tesoriero, "Tree-House Chic: Climb into My Parlor," *Time*, July 22, 2002, Vol. 160 Issue 4, p14; Deborah Baldwin, "The Look of Age, without the Wait," *The New York Times*, August 15, 2002, pD1.

TRANSPORTATION : RVs

Ray Sasser, "Demand for RVs Greater than Ever; Terrorist Attacks Lead Many People to Want to Travel Domestically," *The Dallas Morning News*, February 19, 2002; Robert W. Stock, "Rollin', Rollin', Rollin', Keep Those RV's Rollin'," *The New York Times*, May 7, 2002, Vol. 151 Issue 52111, pE1; Thalia Assuras, "Boomers Hit Road in RVs," *CBS Evening News* (Saturday Edition), May 25, 2002; Jody Snider, "More Newport News, Va., Families Opt to Rent Recreational Vehicles," *Daily Press*, May 26, 2002; Tony Fong, "RV Sales Up Sharply Since Sept. 11, Insiders Say," *The San Diego Union-Tribune*, July 10, 2002; Chris Jones, "Road-Bound Americans Snap Up Recreational Vehicles," *Las Vegas Journal Review*, July 20, 2002; Joe Harwood, "Oregon Rental Agencies See Increase in Popularity of Recreational Vehicles," *The Register Guard*, August 12, 2002; Fred Brock, "Boomers, on the Road Again, Spur Sales of RVs," *The New York Times*, September 1, 2002, Business Section, p10; Erin Burt and Courtney McGrath, "Kings of the Road," *Kiplinger's Personal Finance*, October 2002, Vol. 56 Issue 10, p67.

COOKING : Slow Food

Arlene Coco, "Slow Food Movement Encourages Us All to Slow the Pace of Our Lives," *Duluth News-Tribune*, August 27, 2001; Neil Clark, "Fight Against the Clock," *New Statesman*, June 24, 2002, Vol. 131 Issue 4592, p16; Korva Coleman, "Interview: Monyca Marbach Discusses the Slow Food Baltimore Celebration of Maryland Blue Crabs," *Weekend All Things Considered* (NPR), June 29, 2002; Benjamin Chadwick, "Easy Does It," *E Magazine: The Environmental Magazine*, September/October 2002, Vol. 13 Issue 5, p42.

KITCHEN : Vintage Appliances

Cindy Hoedel, "Happy Days are Here Again in Retro-Inspired Housewares," *The Kansas City Star*, March 14, 2002; Valerie Stivers, "Industrial Revolution," *Time Out New York*, July 25-August 1, 2002, p29; Rachel Emma Silverman, "If a Fridge Has Run for Years, Collectors May be Chasing It," *Wall Street Journal* (Eastern Edition), September 20, 2002, Vol. 240 Issue 58, pA1.

FOOD & BEVERAGE : Classic Cocktails

Jan Stojaspal, "Back in the Bottle," *Time Atlantic*, August 20-27, 2001, Vol. 158 Issue 8, p85; "Bohemia's Brain-Twisting Beverage," *The Moscow Times*, October 11, 2001; Andy Badeker, "The Buzz on Booze, Before Prohibition," *Chicago Tribune*, November 12, 2001; "Drinks News," *Caterer & Hotelkeeper*, January 24, 2002, Vol. 191 Issue 4206, p46; James Scarpa, "Shaking It Up," *Restaurant Business*, May 1, 2002, Vol. 101 Issue 8, p113.

FASHION: Retro Sneakers

Boaz Herzog, "Sneaker Manufacturers Find Gold in Old Styles," *The Oregonian*, July 15, 2002; Crystal Dempsey, "Looking for Retro Sneakers? You'll Find Them a Click Away," *The Charlotte Observer*, July 17, 2002; Tiffany Montgomery, "Nike Plans to Launch Two Skate Shoes in September," *The Orange County Register*, August 21, 2002.

MUSIC: Bluegrass

Ben Ratliff, "Under a Spotlight, the Grass is Still Blue," *The New York Times*, June 18, 2002, Sec. E, p4; Shaun Assael, "Bluegrass's New-Age Hootenanny," *The New York Times*, June 30, 2002, Section 4, p5; Deborah Evans Price and Phyllis Stark, "'O Brother'! Bluegrass is Blooming," *Billboard*, July 20, 2002, Vol. 114 Issue 29, p1.

BUSINESS : Bartering

Jamie Vinson, "Lexington, Ky., Businesses Trade Sign Space for Time on Radio Station," *Lexington Herald-Leader*, April 16, 2002; Matt Krantz, "Regulators Look Closely at Bartering," *USA Today*, May 21, 2002, p3b; Bill Cormier, "Barter is Booming in Argentina," *Associated Press Online*, May 31, 2002; Michelle Leder, "I'll Fix Your Computer if You Paint My Office," *The New York Times*, June 23, 2002, p9 (L); Scott Charton, "Student Trades Pigs for Tuition," *Associated Press Online*, July 26, 2002.